CAMBRIDGE

Time SHOT

AND OTHER STORIES

SUNSHINE COAST
ALTERNATE SCHOOL
BOX 807
SECHELT, B.C. VON 3A0

Judith A. Green

CAMBRIDGE Adult Education
A Division of Simon & Schuster
Upper Saddle River, New Jersey

> *In memory of my aunt*
> *Dorothy Andrews Ferry*

Executive Editor: Mark Moscowitz
Editor: Robert McIlwaine
Production Director: Penny Gibson
Print Buyer: Cheryl Johnson
Production Editor: Linda Greenberg
Book Design: Margarita T. Linnartz
Electronic Page Production: José López
Electronic Art: Armando Baéz and José López
Cover Design: Eric Dawson

Copyright © 1995 by Globe Fearon Educational Publisher, a Division of Simon & Schuster, 1 Lake Street, Upper Saddle River, New Jersey 07458. All rights reserved. No part of this book may be reproduced or transmitted in any form or by any means electrical or mechanical, including photocopying recording, or by any information storage and retrieval system, without permission in writing from the publisher.

Printed in the United States of America
1 2 3 4 5 6 7 8 9 10   99 98 97 96 95

ISBN 0-13-600090-8

CAMBRIDGE Adult Education
A Division of Simon & Schuster
Upper Saddle River, New Jersey

Contents

1. **A LOVE STORY WITH A DOG** 1
   - Comprehension Check 14
   - Reading Tips: Compound Words 16
   - Reading for Background: Dogs............. 17

2. **THE KIDNAPPING OF EDWARD W. THURSTON IV** . 19
   - Comprehension Check 33
   - Reading Tips: Endings (ing and ed) 35
   - Reading for Background: Fingerprints 37

3. **A HOUSE OF THEIR OWN** 39
   - Comprehension Check 51
   - Reading Tips: Endings (er) 54
   - Reading for Background: Floor Plans 56

4. **THE HOUSE THAT WASN'T THERE** 59
   - Comprehension Check 70
   - Reading Tips: Endings (ly and ful) 72
   - Reading for Background: Time Lines 74

5. **COLD WATER** 76
   - Comprehension Check 89
   - Reading Tips: Endings (Change y to i) 91
   - Reading for Background: What Makes the Tides? . 92

6. **TIME SHOT** 96
   - Comprehension Check 110
   - Reading Tips: Endings (y and ness)............ 113
   - Reading for Background: Gravity.............. 114

ANSWERS 117

GLOSSARY 121

To the Instructor

The purpose of this book is primarily to provide an enjoyable reading experience to adult new readers. The six stories revolve around adult interests and experiences; they represent a variety of genres, including suspense, mystery, fantasy, history, human interest, and a ghost story.

The accompanying exercises for each story attempt to draw the student into the range of reading tasks that make up the repertoire of a good reader and that reinforce the concept that the goal of reading is the construction of meaning. These are:

1. Prereading, including self-questioning regarding previously learned background information, and predicting skills;

2. Vocabulary study in dictionary style, along with context-rich illustrating sentences;

3. Vocabulary study sentences that encourage reading in context;

4. A comprehension check, in traditional multiple-choice format, that concentrates on higher-level inferential and judgmental skills;

5. A series of exercises (which may be used in any order or may stand alone) on methods of discovering the meaning of new words through reading in context and use of the dictionary;

6. A short selection of enrichment reading that enhances some aspect of the story line and/or the reading skills exercises; and

7. A set of comprehension questions related to the enrichment reading that also provide practice in finding information which is listed in alphabetical order, including in the dictionary.

An answer key is provided following the last story.

1

A LOVE STORY WITH A DOG

READING IN CONTEXT

Try to figure out the meaning of the word in italics from the words around it.

The Vietnamese children took their grandfather by the hand. "Come with us, *Ong*," they said.

See the answer on page 117.

Before You Read Have you ever known people from another country? Were their ways different from yours? What problems can come up when we are living or working with people whose ways are different?

Mrs. Smith jumped up out of her chair. "That dog is barking again!" she shouted.

Andy got up slowly. His mother was always complaining about something. "What dog? I don't hear a dog," he said.

"That dog upstairs! Those people went out and got a dog! It's bad enough that they have eight people in that tiny apartment. Now, they have a dog, too!"

Andy listened. Yes, now he could hear a dog barking.

"Those people don't belong here!" his mother said. "They can't even speak English! I wish they would go back where they came from!"

"But, Mom, they're from **Vietnam**. There was a war, you know. They *can't* go back."

"Then I wish they would go somewhere else. We don't want them here. Them *or* their dog!"

Andy walked toward the door. "I'll see what I can do about the dog," he said. "I've never been up to their apartment. I'll go talk to them."

"How are you going to talk to them if they don't speak English?" his mother shouted after him.

Andy walked up the stairs from the first floor to the second. He could really hear the dog now, and it *was* barking a lot. The apartment must be very crowded with eight people and a dog in it. Maybe they would move to a bigger place. That would make his mother happy.

He knocked on the door. He could hear voices, all talking at once. He couldn't understand them. They must be speaking Vietnamese, he thought.

The door opened. A young woman was standing in the doorway. She was looking up at him with wide, scared eyes.

She was the most beautiful girl he had ever seen.

She was short, not even up to his shoulder. She had long black hair that hung down her back. Her skin was like cream. When he looked into her eyes, he felt as if he were falling.

The girl didn't say anything. She just stood there and looked up at him. Andy just stood there and looked at her.

Suddenly, there was a noise from inside the room. A little dog came running out into the hall and jumped around Andy, barking. A little boy ran out and grabbed the dog. "Hello," the little boy said. "I'm sorry about the dog. We're trying to teach him not to bark."

Andy turned to look at the little boy. "You speak English!" he said.

"Of course!" the little boy said. "I go to school every day."

"Does *she* speak English?" he asked.

1 • A Love Story With a Dog

The girl smiled. "Yes," she said. "I am Lan. I am glad to meet you. She held out her hand. Andy shook it. It was smooth and tiny and cool. He didn't want to let it go.

"I'm Andy Smith. I live downstairs in the apartment on the first floor."

"As my brother said, we are very sorry about the dog," Lan said. "We got the dog for my grandfather. My grandfather is very old and sad. He does not like it here in America. He does not speak English, and he misses our home in the mountains of Vietnam. We thought the dog might make him happy."

"Yes. Well, that's OK," Andy said.

"Thank you," Lan said. The little boy took the dog back into the apartment. Lan smiled at Andy, then slipped back into the apartment, and closed the door.

Andy went back downstairs. "Well, what happened?" his mother asked as soon as he came in. "Did you tell them to get rid of the dog?"

"They said they'd keep it quiet," Andy said.

"Why didn't you tell them to get rid of it? You should have told them they couldn't keep a dog here. You should have told them you would call the landlord!" Mrs. Smith went on and on.

But Andy wasn't listening. He was trying to think of a way to get to know Lan.

The next morning, Andy kept looking out the window of the apartment.

"What are you doing?" his mother asked.

"Just looking," Andy said.

He waited and waited. He saw the little boy go off to school with two older children. He saw a man go to work. "That must be her father," he thought. A little bit later, a woman left with a girl. Andy looked, but the girl wasn't Lan.

"What are you doing?" Andy's mother asked again. "Aren't you going to work today? You're late!"

Andy looked at the clock. He *was* late! He hurried out the door and across the parking lot to his car.

As he was getting into his car, he looked back. Lan was just coming out of the building.

Andy called to her. "Would you like a ride?"

Lan came over to him. "I am going to work," she said. "I work on Washington Street. Is that the way you are going?"

"It's right on the way," he said as he opened the door for her. "Hop in."

Washington Street was on the other side of the city from the plant where Andy worked. Now he would be *really* late for work. But somehow, with Lan beside him, he didn't care.

In the next few weeks, Andy got to know Lan's family. He took Lan and her mother to the store to buy food. Sometimes, he took the children to school.

One time, they invited him to their apartment for supper. Andy had never been part of a big family. As long as he could remember, it had been just himself and his mother. He liked sitting at the table with all these people, from the grandfather down to the little children. He even liked the dog.

When Lan found out that he worked on the other side of the city, she wouldn't let him take her to work. But sometimes, when he got out of work early, he saw her walking home. Then he would give her a ride. He liked being with her, and he hoped she was glad to see him, too.

He did not dare to tell his mother how he felt. His mother complained every day about Lan's family. She complained about the dog and about the noise of so many people upstairs. She complained about them when they went out and when they came in. She said they slammed the front door and talked too loudly. Andy didn't think that was true, but he didn't dare to say anything.

One day, the grandfather took the dog outside. He sat down on the front steps, and, soon, he fell asleep in the sun. While he was asleep, the dog's leash slipped out of his hand. The dog ran down the steps. In a minute, it had started to dig in Mrs. Smith's flower garden.

Mrs. Smith looked out the window. She saw the dog digging up her beautiful flowers. Then she saw the grandfather on the front steps. He was just sitting there, she thought, watching the dog dig up her flowers.

She went wild with anger.

She ran out of her apartment, down the hall, and out the front door. "Stop it!" she screamed. She pounded on the grandfather's arm. "Make that dog stop it!"

The grandfather woke up with a start. He jumped up and ran down the sidewalk. Then he stopped and looked around him, as if he had just remembered where he was. He looked back at Mrs. Smith, who was still shouting. He looked at his dog and the flowers. He stood still. He seemed to be getting smaller and older.

The children were coming home from school. They saw their grandfather being shouted at. Then they saw the dog in the flowers, and they ran down the street toward the building. The older boy grabbed the dog and picked him up. "Bad dog!" he said. He turned to Mrs. Smith. "We are very sorry for this."

"You should be!" she shouted. "I'm going to complain to the landlord about this! He'll make you get rid of that dog! He should get rid of *you*!"

The boy turned quietly and carried the dog into the building. The other two children took their grandfather by the hand. "Come with us, Ong," they said. They led him up the steps and in the door.

Mrs. Smith didn't see that the old man was crying.

The next morning, when Mrs. Smith looked out her window, there were new flowers in her garden. She didn't care. She went right ahead and called the landlord.

Andy and Lan went for a long walk. It was nice, walking along together in the warm summer night. But they felt very sad.

"My grandfather will not talk to us any more," Lan said. "He just sits and does not look at us."

"Because of the dog and my mother?" Andy asked.

"Yes. He is sad because he let the dog hurt your mother's flowers. But it is more than that, I think. He is sad because your mother shouted at him. He felt like a little child."

"Oh," Andy said.

"He wants to go home," Lan said. "He wants us all to go home."

Andy took her hand and held it. "Do you think you will?"

"No," Lan said. "We can never go home. My father helped the American soldiers in the war. When the American soldiers went away, we had to go away with them. If we had stayed, we would have been killed." Andy squeezed her hand.

"They put us on a ship," Lan went on. "We were on the ship for many days. There was water all around us. We did not know where we were going. We were very much afraid.

"At last, we came to America. We were sent to this city. The people in a church got us this apartment. We were very thankful. But it is still hard. My father and my mother cannot speak English very well. They cannot get good jobs. They work very hard, but they do not earn much money. My grandfather does not speak English at all. He will not try to learn English. He will not go out of the apartment.

"He loves his little dog very much. But now he will not look at his dog. He will not talk to us. He will not eat. Oh, Andy . . ." Lan began to cry. "I am so afraid that my grandfather will die."

1 • A Love Story With a Dog

That night, Andy lay awake for hours. Lan was afraid that her grandfather would die, and it all started with his mother and her stupid flowers.

His mother couldn't stand Lan or her family. Lan's father and mother must really hate his mother and him, he thought.

But he really liked Lan. In fact, he thought he might be falling in love with her.

What was he going to do?

The next day, at his job, Andy worked hard so that he could get done early. As soon as he was done, he hurried out to his car and drove across the city to the store where Lan worked. He parked right in front and waited for her to come out.

Other people came out, but not Lan. Andy waited. Lan still did not come out. Andy went on waiting.

At last, Andy went in. There was almost no one left in the store. Then he saw Lan sitting in the corner, holding her coat. When she saw Andy, she looked down at the floor.

Andy walked over to her. "Hello," he said quietly. "I've come to give you a ride home."

Lan was still looking down at the floor. "That is very nice of you," she said. "But I cannot ride with you."

"You can't ride with me? Why not?"

"My father saw me walking with you last night. My father has said that I must not see you any more."

"But—" Andy started to say. He didn't need to ask her why her father had told her not to see him. He already knew.

He sat down next to her and took her hand. "Lan, do *you* want to see me?" he asked softly.

Lan turned her face away. "Yes. But I must do what my father says." She pulled her hand away from his. Then she got up and walked out of the store. She did not look back.

The next few weeks were the worst weeks in Andy's life.

When Lan's brothers and sisters went to school, they hurried away from the apartment building. They did not stop to say hello to Andy.

Lan's father and mother would not speak to him when they saw him on the front steps.

He never saw Lan at all.

His mother went right on complaining. She complained about the dog and the children and the noise. She complained to Andy. She called the landlord to complain. "They shouldn't have that dog," she told Andy. "Any day now, the landlord will come over. He told me he would come. He'll make them get rid of that dog. Maybe he'll make them all move. It's not that I have anything against people from Vietnam. It's just that there are too many people in that little apartment. The landlord should never have let them move in. . . ." She went on and on.

Andy went to talk to his boss. The company he worked for had plants in three other cities. Andy asked his boss if he could move to a job in a **plant** in another city.

"You're not happy here?" his boss asked.

"The company is fine. I'm just having some problems at home," Andy said.

"I understand," his boss said. "I'll try to find you something. It will take a few weeks."

"Thank you," Andy said. "I'll take anything. I just want to get out of here."

Lan was sad, too.

She went to work. She came home. She helped with the housework. But she almost never spoke.

The grandfather was sad and quiet. He would not eat. He was becoming thin and weak.

With Lan and the grandfather so quiet and sad, the whole family began to feel sad. Even the children were quiet.

The dog ran from one person to the next, but no one wanted to play with him. When he sat down by the grandfather, the grandfather just put his hand on the dog's head. His hand was so thin now. He just sat and looked at the wall.

Lan sat and looked out the window.

The clock on the wall ticked loudly.

One day, it all changed.

The day started like any other day. Andy went to work. Lan and her mother and father went to work. The children went to school.

The grandfather sat in the apartment, his hand on the dog's head, looking at the wall.

Andy's mother cleaned her apartment. She kept looking out the window to make sure that the dog was not in her flowers.

It was time for the mail to come. Mrs. Smith headed for the front door to see if there was any mail for her. But suddenly, she stopped. She had such a pain in her head! It hurt so much! She must get help! She took another step toward the door and another. . . . She reached for the door. . . . The pain! Her head hurt so much! She felt dizzy. She fell to the floor.

She had never been so scared in her life.

She couldn't move her left leg or her arm.

She began to cry.

Upstairs, the dog's ears went up. He began to move around. He went over to the door and back to the grandfather's chair. He pushed his nose against the grandfather's hand. The grandfather did not move.

The dog went back to the door. He barked one sharp bark. Then he looked back at the grandfather. The grandfather was still looking at the wall.

Downstairs, Mrs. Smith was still crying. But she was crying more softly now. The pain was so great, and she was growing weaker.

Upstairs, the dog barked again. He barked short, sharp barks again and again. Then he ran over to the grandfather and pushed his head up under the old man's hand.

Slowly, the grandfather turned his head to look at the dog.

The dog ran back to the door, barking those short, sharp barks. The grandfather looked at him.

Slowly, the grandfather stood up.

He walked slowly to the dog. Slowly, he reached up and got the leash and put it on the dog. Slowly, he opened the door. Then, step by slow step, he went down the stairs to the first floor.

He started to go outside. But the dog pulled at the leash and pulled the grandfather over to Mrs. Smith's door.

The grandfather shook his head. He tried to pull the dog over to the outside door. But the dog wouldn't move. He began to bark again.

The grandfather began to worry. Any moment now, he thought, Mrs. Smith would burst out of her door and shout at him. He tried to get the dog to be quiet. He bent down and put his hand on the dog's head and tried to push him away from the door.

Then he heard it. Mrs. Smith's voice, soft and weak, calling for help.

He called out to her. She heard him, and she called back as loudly as she could, "Help me! Please help me! I can't move! I'm dying. Help me! Please help me! Please help me!"

The grandfather couldn't understand what she was saying, but he knew that something was wrong. He tried to open her door, but it was locked.

What should he do? How could he get help? He hurried out of the door and down to the sidewalk, the dog running along beside him. But there was no one around.

He hurried over to the next building. He rang the doorbell to the first apartment and then the second. Then he rang the doorbells for all the apartments.

No one came.

He hurried on to the next building. He rang all the doorbells at once. At last, upstairs, a young woman came to the door. "What do you want?" she called down the stairs.

The grandfather hurried up the stairs. He took the young woman by the hand and tried to pull her with him down the stairs. But she pulled her hand away from him. "What are you doing, old man?" she asked him. "Who are you?"

The grandfather clasped his hands in front of him. How could he get her to understand?

He had to remember! He had to remember what Mrs. Smith had said!

He said his first words in English: "Please help me."

The young woman looked at him. Then she said, "Just a minute." She went back inside her apartment. The grandfather waited. Would she come back? Then her door opened again, and she came out, holding a little boy by the hand.

The grandfather led them down the stairs, out the door, and down the sidewalk to his own building. The dog ran along beside them, barking. The grandfather led them into the front hall, up to Mrs. Smith's door. He pointed at the door.

"What's wrong?" the young woman asked. "Are you locked out?"

The grandfather put his ear to the door and waved for the young woman to do the same. Now, she could hear it: a faint, weak voice saying, "Oh, please, please help me."

The young woman called out, "We'll help you!" She tried the door, but she couldn't open it. She turned to the grandfather. "Do you have a phone?"

The old man just looked at her sadly. What was she asking him?

Cambridge Reader

The young woman moved her hands like someone using a phone. Now, he understood! The grandfather nodded his head yes. He pulled at the woman to get her to come up the stairs.

The woman called to Mrs. Smith, "We're going to get help. We'll be right back." Then she took her little boy by the hand and followed the grandfather up to his apartment. Quickly, she called 911 and asked the police to send an **ambulance** right away.

In a few minutes, the ambulance came. The grandfather showed the **rescue** workers to Mrs. Smith's door. "Hello!" they called to her. "This is the Rescue. Can you open the door?"

"No. . . ." came the tiny, weak voice. "I can't move my leg."

"We're going to have to break down the door," the rescue worker said. "Get ready!" One of them ran back to the rescue van for an ax. Soon they split the door open. One of the rescue workers reached in and unlocked it.

As soon as the door was open, the grandfather hurried into the apartment. There was Mrs. Smith, lying on the floor. The grandfather bent down and took her hand.

"It was you, wasn't it?" Mrs. Smith said. "Thank you, oh, thank you."

The rescue workers checked Mrs. Smith carefully. "It looks as if she has had a stroke," they told the grandfather. The old man could only look at them.

The rescue workers turned to the young woman. "She'll be all right. It will take some time, but she'll be all right. It's a good thing you found her so soon. Is she your mother?"

The young woman just smiled. "No, I live down the street." She pointed at the grandfather. "I think she's a friend of his," she said.

1 • A Love Story With a Dog

The rescue workers loaded Mrs. Smith into the ambulance. They called Andy at work, and he hurried to the hospital to be with his mother. All that day, he sat next to her bed.

She didn't say anything to him. It was very hard for her to talk. She just lay still in the bed, holding his hand. Sometimes, he could see that she was crying.

Late in the afternoon, Andy heard someone come quietly into the room. When he turned around, he saw the grandfather standing there. Behind the grandfather, there was Lan and her father.

The grandfather came up to the bed where Mrs. Smith was lying. Mrs. Smith held out her hand to him and smiled.

Andy sat there. He was too surprised to say a word.

Lan told him, "It was my grandfather and his dog who found your mother this morning. It was my grandfather who got help for her."

Andy looked at the grandfather. "Please tell him thank you," he told Lan.

Then he looked at the father. Lan's father was smiling at him.

Then he looked at Lan.

She was smiling at him, too.

Mrs. Smith was in the hospital for two months. Then the doctors said she could come home.

She still has a hard time walking, but she is slowly getting better. Andy has kept his job in the city so that he can look after her.

Andy and Lan are planning to get married in the spring. Mrs. Smith and Lan's mother are looking forward to the time when they will be grandmothers.

Lan's grandfather still has his dog. The dog is growing very fat because Mrs. Smith gives him treats to eat every time she sees him.

Cambridge Reader

The grandfather is trying to learn to speak a little English. He wants to speak well enough so that he can use the phone. Just in case.

Comprehension Check

Pick the best answer for each question.

1. In the beginning of the story, you could tell that Mrs. Smith

    a. didn't speak English.

    b. got along well with everyone.

    c. liked to complain about everything.

    d. wished that she could speak Vietnamese.

2. In the beginning of the story, Andy went upstairs to talk to the Vietnamese family about their dog. Why didn't he shout at them to get rid of the dog?

    a. He couldn't find anyone who could speak English.

    b. He didn't know they had a dog.

    c. His mother wanted him to be nice to them.

    d. He was attracted to the daughter in the family.

3. Andy gave Lan a ride home from work in his car because

    a. he wanted to be with her.

    b. he worked in the same place she did.

c. he felt sorry for her because she didn't make very much money.

   d. she was too old to walk very far.

4. Lan's family had to leave Vietnam because

   a. they were afraid that they couldn't find a place to live after the war.

   b. some people in Vietnam hated them for helping the American side in the war.

   c. some people hated them for helping the Vietnamese side in the war.

   d. they were afraid of the American soldiers in Vietnam.

5. At first, the grandfather didn't learn to speak English because

   a. he couldn't hear well enough.

   b. he didn't want to live in America.

   c. he didn't know anyone who could speak English.

   d. his family thought he was too old to learn.

6. Why did Andy ask his boss for a job at another plant?

   a. He was mad at his mother because her complaining made it so that he couldn't see Lan any more.

   b. He was mad at the Vietnamese family because their dog kept barking.

   c. He was mad at Lan because he thought she was in love with someone else.

   d. He was mad at his boss because he wouldn't let Andy go home early.

Cambridge Reader

7. How did the grandfather know that Mrs. Smith needed help?

   a. She called him on the phone.

   b. He heard her calling out the window.

   c. The dog heard her crying and got him to come.

   d. The dog saw her fall and got him to come.

8. The grandfather helped Mrs. Smith because

   a. he wanted her to like Lan.

   b. he wanted her to like his dog.

   c. she was a person, and she needed help.

   d. she had helped him when he needed help.

Answers are on page 117.

Reading Tips: Compound Words

Some longer words are made up of two smaller words, like this:

something	=	some	+	thing
upstairs	=	up	+	stairs
maybe	=	may	+	be

Look at the words listed on the next page. Can you match the words on the left side with the words on the right

16

side to make longer words from the story? The first one is done for you.

in	father
grand	noon
after	side
land	thing
side	lord
any	walk

Answers are on page 117.

READING FOR BACKGROUND:

Dogs

Dogs are called "man's best friend." People and dogs have been friends for a long time . . . about 20,000 years! Cave men kept dogs to help them track animals when they went hunting.

For thousands of years, people have kept dogs for hunting, for looking after sheep, as watchdogs, and as pets. Dogs are also used to help the police or to lead people who are blind. They can also pull small carts and sleds.

A dog can hear sounds that are too high for people to hear. They can also hear sounds about ten times as far away as we can.

Dogs are known for their sense of smell. They can tell what something is by its smell, the same way we can tell what it is by looking at it. In the mountains, dogs can find people who are lost in the snow. In fact, dogs have found people who were buried under 20 feet of snow!

Dogs can't see as well as people can. For instance, they can't see colors. A dog can see something better if it is moving. It sees things by their brightness more than by their shape.

Cambridge Reader

Dogs come in all shapes and sizes. There are more than 100 breeds of dogs. Look at this chart to find out more about these breeds.

When you look *across* a row, you will find out more about one breed of dog. When you look *down* the chart, you can see how the breeds are different from each other.

Name	Weight	Height (at the shoulder)
Chihuahua	1 to 6 pounds	5 inches
Cocker spaniel	22 to 28 pounds	14 to 15 inches
Collie	50 to 75 pounds	22 to 26 inches
Saint Bernard	165 to 180 pounds	25 to 30 inches
Irish wolfhound	105 to 140 pounds	30 to 34 inches

Use the chart to answer these questions.

1. What is the weight of a collie?

   _____

2. What is the height of a cocker spaniel?

   _____

3. What is the smallest breed of dog in the chart?

   _____

4. What breed of dog weighs the most?

   _____

5. What breed of dog is the tallest?

   _____

Answers are on page 117.

2 THE KIDNAPPING OF EDWARD W. THURSTON IV

READING IN CONTEXT

Try to figure out the meaning of the word in italics from the words around it. (The word is the numeral "IV.")

Edward W. Thurston *IV* was the son of Edward W. Thurston III, one of the richest men in the United States.

See the answer on page 117.

Before You Read How would you feel if your child was kidnapped? If *you* were kidnapped, what would you do? Would you try to get away or just wait and hope?

Ever since he was born, Edward W. Thurston IV had always had everything he wanted. His father, Edward W. Thurston III, was one of the richest men in the United States, so anything that Edward IV wanted, he got.

His life had its problems, too. When Edward IV was born, his father knew that he would have to be very careful. Someone might kidnap the baby to try to get money from the Thurstons. Mr. Thurston hired guards to protect the baby.

If the maid took the baby to the park, a guard went, too. At night, two guards watched the Thurstons's house.

The maid slept outside the baby's door. Even as Edward grew older, he always had a guard with him. When he grew old enough to go to school, a guard went, too.

No one knew how the kidnappers got into the house in the night. All they knew was that on the morning of his seventh birthday, Edward IV was not there.

When the maid went into his room to wake him, his bed was empty. The maid ran to get Mrs. Thurston. Mrs. Thurston screamed for Mr. Thurston. Mr. Thurston called the guards. They looked everywhere, but they couldn't find the boy.

Mrs. Thurston was crying. "What will we do?" she kept asking.

"We will wait," Mr. Thurston said.

When Edward had gone to bed that night, he was very happy, thinking about his birthday the next day. In the middle of the night, he woke up in the dark. Someone was in the room with him. He thought it was the maid, checking the window. Then a hand came down on his mouth, hard. "If you make a sound," a voice said in his ear, "we will kill you." Someone pushed something into his mouth and tied something over his face. He could hardly breathe! Someone else tied his arms and legs. Then they picked him up and pushed him through the window.

Edward could feel the cool night air. Where were the guards? He wanted his mother and father! The men were running with him. They put him up over the wall that was around the yard. A car was waiting on the street. They threw him into the trunk and shut the lid, and the car drove quickly away.

It seemed as if he was in the trunk for a long time. The ropes hurt his arms and legs. The thing in his mouth made it hard to breathe. Edward cried for his mother. But when he was crying, it was even harder to breathe. At last, gasping for breath, he fainted.

He woke up in a room, in the dark. His arms and legs were free. The thing was out of his mouth. He was on a bed.

But it was not his bed.

2 • The Kidnapping of Edward W. Thurston IV

He lay curled up on the bed, in the dark, and cried.

All that day, the boy's mother and father waited for a call from the kidnappers. At last, late in the evening, the call came.

When the phone rang, Mr. Thurston picked it up. "Is this Edward W. Thurston *the third*?" a cold voice asked.

"Yes," Mr. Thurston said.

"Do you want your boy back?" the voice asked.

"Yes! Of course! I want my son home safe. What do you want?"

"We want $10 million," the voice said, "in small bills."

"*$10 million!*" Mr. Thurston shouted. "Now, look here—"

"We know you have it," the voice said. "Isn't your boy worth that much?"

"Yes! But if you know I have it, you also know that I don't have that much money in cash! My money is tied up in land and buildings!"

"Sell them," the voice said.

"But if I try to sell them fast, I won't get as much money for them!" Mr. Thurston shouted. "I can't raise $10 million right away!"

"We can wait," the voice said. "But we won't wait for long."

"How do I *know* you have my son?" Mr. Thurston asked.

"We can prove we have him."

"Don't hurt him!" Mr. Thurston said.

"Then get the money! $10 million. And get it fast! And one more thing: Don't go to the police. If you do, things won't go well for your son."

The phone went dead.

Edward lay in the dark for a long time. Some of the time, he was awake. Some of the time, he was asleep. Some of the time, he couldn't tell.

Suddenly he heard footsteps. A door opened, letting in a flash of light. It was so bright! Then the door closed again. A man came toward him, holding a flashlight. The flashlight shone on the floor and on a dirty brick wall. There was nothing in the room but the bed, Edward, and the man. "I brought you some food, kid," the man said.

"I'm not hungry!" Edward said. "I want to go home!"

"You're not going home until we get our money from your father," the man said. "So you'd better eat this." He put a paper bag down on the bed beside Edward.

"But—I need to go to the bathroom!" Edward said.

"I'll get you a can," the man said. He left the room. A minute later, he came back and put a can down on the floor. "Now give me your shirt."

"My shirt?"

"Yes, your pajama shirt." The man held out his hand. Edward looked down at his pajama shirt, which had *EWT IV* on the pocket. Edward pulled it off and gave it to the man. The man turned to walk away.

"Wait!" Edward called. "It's dark! I want a light!"

"No! No lights!" The man went out and closed the door behind him. Edward could hear a key turning in the lock. The footsteps went away. Then it was quiet.

Edward curled up on the bed and cried.

At the Thurstons's house, another long, slow, sad day went by.

The phone rang. Mr. Thurston grabbed it. "Hello? Hello?"

"You wanted proof that we have your son," the voice said. "You will get your son's pajama shirt in the mail today. Now, listen, and listen good. We will call you tomorrow to tell you where to leave the money. Ten million dollars, in small bills."

"But—" Mr. Thurston started to say.

"*Get the money!*" the voice said. The line went dead.

Edward sat on the bed, eating a sandwich. That's all they ever gave him to eat: sandwiches. He was tired of sandwiches. More than anything, he was tired of being in the dark. He put down the sandwich and started to cry.

Suddenly, he heard a voice. "Hey, you!" it said. "Why are you crying?"

Edward stopped crying and looked around. Where was the voice coming from? It didn't sound like the man who brought him the sandwiches. It sounded like a boy. "Where are you?" he asked.

"Right here," the voice said. "On the other side of the wall." Edward heard a tapping sound near his head. "I keep hearing someone crying. Who are you?" the voice asked. "Why are you crying?"

"I'm Edward W. Thurston IV," Edward said. "I'm crying because I've been locked up in the dark, and I don't even know where I am."

"You're in an old, empty building," the voice said. "How did you get in there?"

"I've been kidnapped."

"Kidnapped?" the voice said. "Naw. You couldn't be kidnapped. Are you being punished for something?"

"No! I tell you, I've been kidnapped!" Edward said.

"Naw. You're making it up," the voice said. "I'm out of here."

"Wait! Hello? Hello?" Edward called.

No one answered him.

Edward was crying again. He was more lonely than ever. Suddenly, he heard the voice again.

"Hey! Hey, you! Eddie!"

Edward stopped crying. "Hello!" he said.

"Hey, Eddie, how old are you?" the voice asked.

"I'm seven."

"You're only seven? They've sure kept you in there an awful long time. Are they giving you anything to eat?"

"Yes, but it's just sandwiches and water. But I just wish they'd let me have a light."

"They're keeping you in the *dark*?" the boy's voice asked.

"Yes. I *told* you." In spite of himself, Edward started to cry again.

"Hey, don't cry," the voice said. "Look, like I told you, you're in an old, empty building. No one has used it for years. I like to play out back here. That's how I heard you crying. Anyway, I went around to the front of the building. There's no one around. But there's a big padlock on the door. That wasn't there before."

"I *told* you," Edward said.

"Look, I can't do anything about the padlock," the voice said. "I tried. But maybe I can loosen up a brick or something. Then you can have some light."

"OK," Edward said.

"Stand back." There was a tap-tap-tap on the wall, all in different places. At last, the boy found what he was looking for. One brick, down low, was a little bit loose. Tap, tap, tap, tap. He hit it again and again. Suddenly, it moved. Bit by bit, he pushed it into the room, and a spot of light shone on the floor. That little spot of light looked so beautiful to Edward.

"Oh, thank you!" Edward said. He lay down on the floor and looked through the hole. He could see a yard, full of trash. Farther away, there were other brick walls. Near to him, he could see part of a face, and one big, brown eye. "What's your name?" Edward asked. "How old are you?"

"My name is Willie," the other boy said. "I'm ten. Now, listen to me, Eddie," he added. "Don't leave that brick out of the

2 • The Kidnapping of Edward W. Thurston IV

hole. If *they* find that hole, they'll punish you. If you hear them coming, put it back in. Always be ready."

"OK, Willie," Edward said.

"Wait! I hear a car!" Willie jumped to his feet. "Put the brick back in the hole!" He was already running away.

Quickly, Edward grabbed the brick. He could hear footsteps coming through the building. He tried to push the brick into the hole. It wouldn't go in all the way. He pulled it out again and tried it the other way up. He could hear the key turning in the lock on his door. He pushed and pushed on the brick. It still wasn't all the way in. There wasn't any more time! Just as the door opened, he rolled away from the wall.

The man with the flashlight came into the room. He shined the light on the bed. Then he shined it around the floor until he found Edward. "Hey, kid!" he said. "What are you doing on the floor? Don't you like the nice bed we got you?"

Edward didn't answer. He was still too scared to speak.

"Well, here are your sandwiches, kid. See you again tomorrow." The man left the room and locked the door behind him. Edward could hear him walking away through the building.

Edward waited for a long time to be sure the man had gone away. Then he pulled the brick out of the wall.

He looked and looked through the hole. The yard looked beautiful to him. He watched the light change as the sun moved across the sky.

He was almost happy as he waited for Willie.

Another day went by. Mr. and Mrs. Thurston were waiting by the phone. Mrs. Thurston was holding Edward's pajama shirt in her lap. From time to time, she patted it. She kept crying, softly.

When the phone rang, Mr. Thurston grabbed it. "Hello? Hello?"

"Do you have the money?" the voice asked.

"No! Not all of it! I told you I can't raise that much money that fast. I've only got $3 million. Please! Take that and give us our son back!"

"No. It has to be $10 million," the voice said. "What do we need to do to make you understand that?"

"Don't hurt him! Please! He's only seven years old!"

"He's just fine. So far. You have two more days."

The phone went dead.

Mr. Thurston turned to his wife. "We have to go to the police," he said.

Edward heard Willie's tap on the wall. Quickly, he lay down on the floor and pulled the brick out of the wall. "Hi, Willie!"

"Hey, Eddie! Are you Eddie *Thurston*?"

"I'm Edward W. Thurston IV."

"It *is* you! You're in all the newspapers! You're on TV! You *have* been kidnapped!" Willie said.

"I *told* you. My father will give the kidnappers some money, and then they will let me go home. Right?"

Willie shook his head. "It said on the TV that the kidnappers want $10 million!"

"Well," Edward said, smiling, "my father is very rich."

"Eddie, $10 million is a lot of money. A *lot* of money. It said on the TV that your father can't get that much money."

Edward's smile began to go away as he thought about this. "What will happen to me?" he asked. Then he smiled again. "I know! It doesn't matter about the money. I'll give you my phone number. Then you can call my father, and he'll come and get me."

"But then the kidnappers might get *him*!"

"Not if he brings the police with him," Edward said.

"I'll give it a try," Willie said.

2 • The Kidnapping of Edward W. Thurston IV

The phone rang. Mr Thurston reached for it, but a policeman waved him away. The policeman picked up the phone. "Hello?" he said.

"Is Mr. Thurston there?" a small voice said.

"What do you want?" the policeman asked.

"I know where his son is."

"How do we know you're telling the truth? What proof do you have?" the policeman asked.

"Proof?"

"Look, little boy, we're getting lots of calls every day from people like you. This isn't funny. We're waiting for a call. If you have something to say, take it to the police."

"But I— Oh!" The phone went dead.

The policeman hung up the phone. "Who was it?" Mrs. Thurston asked.

"Another kid, just trying to be funny," the policeman said. "Don't let it worry you."

Edward's father tried every way he knew to get more money. He found someone who said he would buy some more land. He made a deal to borrow some money. But that only made $5 million. He was still only halfway there.

The police were looking for Edward. They called in the FBI. But they didn't know where to look. Edward was just gone.

What would happen? The kidnappers must know that the Thurstons had called the police. Now, the two days were almost up. Would the kidnappers kill Edward?

Time was running out.

Willie pushed something through the hole to Edward. "Eat this," he said.

Edward looked at it. It was a candy bar! He tore the paper off it and bit into it. It tasted so good! "Thank you!" Edward said. "Did you call my father?"

"I tried. No one would listen to me. They said it wasn't funny. Then I thought I saw one of the men coming, so I hung up."

"Oh, no!

"Listen, Eddie, it said on the TV that your father still can't come up with the money. We've got to get you out of there. I've got some tools. Maybe we can get some more bricks out of this wall. Maybe we can make the hole bigger."

"But what about the man with the flashlight? He comes a lot now, three or four times a day."

"I think the kidnappers are getting nervous, too. They don't like all this news about you on TV and in the newspapers. We'll have to work fast."

"Oh, Willie, I want to go home," Edward said.

They worked as much as they dared. They had to keep stopping to listen for the kidnappers.

They got another brick out of the wall, then another, and another. Each time, they were careful to put it back into place. They didn't want the man with the flashlight to see the hole.

Now, they had eight bricks loose. When they took out all the bricks, the hole was almost big enough for Edward to get through.

"Hey! I hear someone!" Willie said. "Quick! Give me your tools!"

Edward pushed his tools out through the hole. "Run, Willie!" he said. "Run! If they catch you—"

"They won't catch me," Willie said. "But I've got to go anyway. It's getting dark. Come on! Get those bricks back in the hole! I'll see you tomorrow! Good-bye!"

Quickly, Edward started to put the bricks back into the hole. Five bricks were in, six bricks, seven.... Suddenly, he heard the key turning in the door. There was no time to put the last brick back! Just as the door opened, Edward sat down with his back to the wall, covering the hole.

The man came into the room. Edward sat still, hoping that the man wouldn't make him stand up. But the man just stood there with the flashlight, shining it around and around the room.

"There's something going on here," the man said at last. "I don't know what it is, but I'm going to find out. There's just something funny going on."

The flashlight stopped. It was shining on the floor. It was shining on a piece of paper.

"That's from a candy bar!" the man said. "Where did you get a candy bar? I didn't bring it to you. Tell me! Where did you get it?"

"I—I had it!" Edward said. "I had it in my pocket."

"You had it in your—?" The man was walking slowly toward him. "No, I don't think so. There's something going on here." Suddenly, he grabbed Edward and pulled him away from the wall. "What's this?" he shouted. He shined the flashlight on the hole where that one last brick was missing. "You've been working on this wall, haven't you? Someone has been helping you, too. You couldn't do it without tools. That someone brought you the candy bar." He grabbed Edward and shook him. "Who was it? Who?"

"I—I—I don't know!" Edward said.

"Well, we're going to find out," the man said. "We'll *get* him! But first we're going to get you out of here!" the man said. "We'll put you somewhere so far away and so dark that no one will *ever* find you! If your father doesn't come up with that money by tomorrow, no one will ever see you alive again!" The man threw Edward down on the bed. "I'll be back! Soon!" he said. The man went out of the room and slammed the door and locked it. Edward heard his footsteps hurrying through the building.

Edward was too scared to cry. He just lay on the bed in the dark, waiting, waiting for the man to come back.

Suddenly, there was a sound. It was a tapping sound and then the sound of a brick hitting the floor.

"Eddie!" a voice called quietly. "Eddie!"

Edward jumped up from the bed. "Willie! Is that you? I thought you were gone!"

"I heard what the man said, so I hid in the yard until he left. Come on! We don't have much time! Help me get these bricks out."

Edward pulled at the loose bricks. As fast as he could, he pulled them out onto the floor. But the hole was still too small.

"Come on, Eddie! Come through the hole!" Willie called.

"It's too small! I'll get stuck! Take some more bricks out," Edward said.

"We don't have time to get them loose! Come on!"

Edward put his head through the hole, then his arms, and then one shoulder. The other shoulder got stuck. Willie grabbed his arms and pulled, but Edward didn't move.

Edward's legs and feet were still in the room. He tried to pull himself back in, but now he couldn't move at all.

Suddenly, Willie jumped. "I hear a car!" he said. "They're coming back!"

"Run, Willie!" Edward said. "Get away, or they'll get you, too!"

"No! I'm not going without you!"

Willie pulled on Edward's arms. Edward felt as if his arms were going to come off. He could hear the men coming through the building. At any moment, they would be grabbing his feet!

Suddenly, he began to move. His pajamas were ripping. One more brick was coming loose. He wiggled and pushed and strained, and Willie pulled. Then all at once, Edward was falling out of the hole, out into the night. He fell in a pile on top of Willie.

Just then, the men came into the room. The light flashed around the room. "Hey!" they shouted. "Where are you?" Then the light found the hole. "He's gone! He got out!"

Willie jumped up and pulled Edward to his feet. "Run!" he told Edward. "Run!" He pulled Edward with him across the yard.

The men ran to the hole in the wall. They shined the flashlight through it. "There they are!" one of the men shouted. "Get them!"

Willie and Edward ran and ran—around the next building—down the street—around another building—across another street—through a door and down some steps. Willie pulled Edward into a basement room. It was full of old trash. They hid in an empty box in the corner. They were out of breath, shaking with fear, so tired from running. They didn't dare say a word.

Now, they heard shouts and running footsteps. Would the men come down the steps? No, they went by. Everything was quiet.

Willie and Edward still did not dare move. They stayed in the box for a long, long time.

At last, they got up. Quietly, they got out of the box and then went up the stairs. They looked up and down the street. There was no one around.

Willie took Edward by the hand, and they began to walk. They kept away from the streetlights. They didn't want anyone to see them, two little boys, one in nothing but dirty pajama pants, on the street in the middle of the night.

At last, they came to the police station. Willie pushed Edward up the steps. "You go in," he said.

"Aren't you coming in with me?" Edward asked.

"No," Willie said. "I've got to get home. My mother must be worried sick. She's going to be really mad at me."

"But you've got to come in! You saved me! My father is rich. He'll give you a reward. He'll put you in the newspapers and on TV. Then *everyone* will know you saved me!"

Willie bent down to look Edward in the face. "Look, Eddie, I'm really glad you're safe. I couldn't stand it when you were in that dark room. But I don't want a reward. And I don't want to be on TV. I don't want to have to worry about those men being after *me*. I like things just the way they are." He gave Edward a quick hug. "Now, I've got to get home. You go on in." He pushed Edward toward the door of the police station.

Edward looked at the door. He could see lights inside. They looked so good! "But, Willie—" he started to say. He turned around to look at him.

Willie was gone. The street was dark and empty.

Edward took a deep breath. He opened the door to the police station and walked in. "I think you're looking for me," he said to the surprised man behind the desk. "I'm Edward W. Thurston IV."

Edward never saw Willie again.

The police found the building where Edward had been locked up. But the kidnappers were never caught.

Edward's father bought the building where Edward had been. He had it torn down, took away all the trash, and built a big new playground. Edward hoped Willie liked it. He wasn't sure he would. He never saw him there.

Even years later, when he had grown up, Edward remembered Willie. Sometimes, he would have his driver drive him up and down those streets. He would look at the people on the sidewalk, looking for Willie.

He never found him.

Comprehension Check

Pick the best answer for each question.

1. Which of these things must have happened *first*?
   a. The kidnappers took Edward to the empty building.
   b. The kidnappers got into the Thurston's house.
   c. The kidnappers planned the kidnapping.
   d. The kidnappers called the Thurstons on the phone.

2. Why didn't Edward's father pay the kidnappers right away?
   a. He had to sell his land and buildings to get the money.
   b. He didn't think that Edward had really been kidnapped.
   c. He didn't care about Edward.
   d. He was hoping that Edward would get away.

3. The kidnappers took Edward's shirt because
   a. they wanted him to be cold.
   b. they wanted to destroy it.
   c. they were going to send it to his mother and father to show that they had kidnapped him.
   d. they were going to send it to his mother and father so that they would think he was dead.

Cambridge Reader

4. Mrs. Thurston was holding Edward's pajama shirt on her lap and crying. Why did she hold the shirt if it made her sad?

   a. She was mad because the shirt was dirty.

   b. She was the kind of person who likes to be sad.

   c. It made her think that Edward was at home again.

   d. It made her feel closer to her son.

5. There were many reasons why Willie helped Edward. Which one of these is *not* a reason why Willie helped Edward?

   a. He wanted a reward from Edward's father.

   b. He felt sorry for Edward because he was so little.

   c. He thought it would be fun to try to outsmart the kidnappers.

   d. He thought kidnapping was wrong.

6. Why did the kidnappers start checking on Edward many times each day?

   a. They knew that Edward was trying to get away.

   b. They were nervous because a lot of people knew that Edward had been kidnapped.

   c. They had seen Willie around the building where they were keeping Edward.

   d. They were nervous because they thought Edward was getting sick.

7. Why didn't Willie want anyone to know that he had helped Edward to get away?

   a. He was afraid of the kidnappers.

b. He was afraid of Edward's father.

   c. He thought that his mother would be mad at him.

   d. He didn't like newspapers or TV news.

8. Why did Edward think Willie wouldn't like the new playground?

   a. He knew Willie didn't like to play.

   b. He knew that Willie didn't like anyone.

   c. Willie seemed to want to stay away from rich people.

   d. Willie seemed to like playing around the old buildings.

Answers are on page 118.

Reading Tips: Endings (ing and ed)

Long words are sometimes made up of a shorter word and an *ending.* Look at these words:

looking = look + ing
seemed = seem + ed

Each ending has a meaning. The *ing* ending means that something *is* or *was* happening. The *ed* ending means that something *already* happened. Look at these sentences:

<u>Right now</u>, he <u>look**ing**</u> out the window.
<u>A little while ago</u>, he <u>look**ed**</u> out the window.

35

Cambridge Reader

There are a few rules about putting on endings. If a word ends with an e, you take off the e before you put on the ending.

hire ⟶ hir

+ ing ⟶ hiring

+ ed ⟶ hired

If the word ends with one vowel and one consonant, most of the time you have to double the consonant before you put on the ending.

tap ⟶ tap + p

+ ing ⟶ tapping

+ ed ⟶ tapped

You don't have to worry about these rules while you are reading. Just go ahead and read the word and the ending, and remember to think about the meaning. You only have to worry about these rules when you are writing.

Put the right word in each blank.

hiring
hired

1. When Edward was a baby, his father _____ guards to protect him.

gasping
gasped

2. Edward can't breathe. He is _____ for breath.

waiting
waited

3. A car was _____ on the street.

shouting
shouted

4. Mr. Thurston _____ into the phone, "Don't hurt my son!"

turning
turned

5. The man _____ the key in the lock.

tiring   **6.** It is very _____ to cry for a
tired   long time.

Answers are on page 118.

READING FOR BACKGROUND:
Fingerprints

The police and the FBI often use *fingerprints* as a way to *identify* someone, or find out who the person is.

No two fingerprints are the same. Even on the same person, each finger has a different fingerprint. Even people who are twins, and look just alike, have different fingerprints. Also, a person's fingerprints never change. They are the same all of his life. So if a fingerprint is found, the police can tell who made it.

First, there has to be a record of the person's fingerprints. The fingerprints are put on a card. Ink is put on the fingers, and all ten fingers are rolled on the card to make the prints.

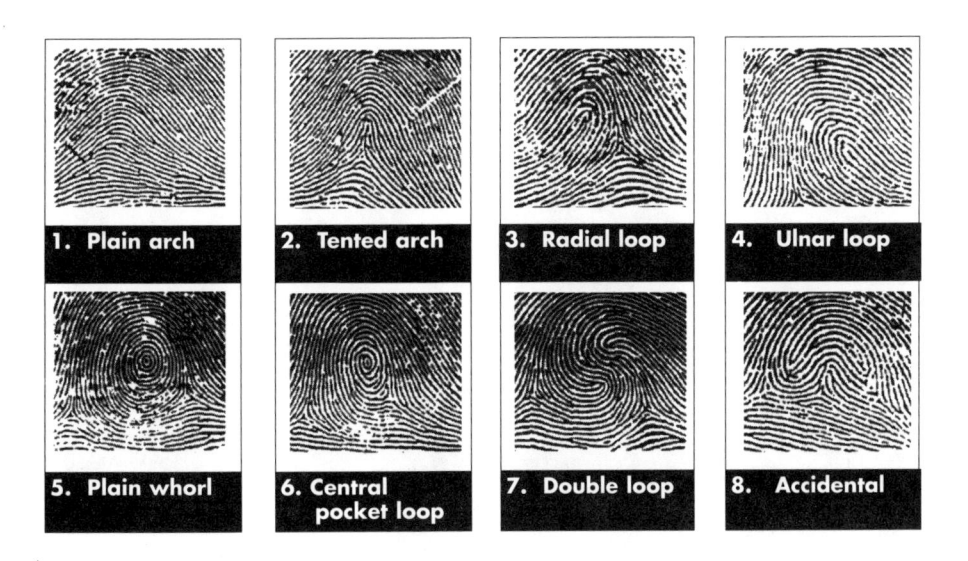

1. Plain arch
2. Tented arch
3. Radial loop
4. Ulnar loop
5. Plain whorl
6. Central pocket loop
7. Double loop
8. Accidental

Cambridge Reader

The police have been using fingerprints since 1896. If a person has touched something smooth and left a fingerprint while committing a crime, the police can find out who did it. The police also use fingerprints to identify people who are missing from their families. Fingerprints have also been used to identify people who have lost their memories.

The FBI has cards with millions and millions of fingerprints. Fingerprints can be put into eight different groups, or types. The cards with the same types are kept together. Then the FBI can find the card they want in just a few minutes.

1. Look at the chart of the different types of fingerprints. How many of them have some kind of *loop*?
2. In this chart, which number is the *ulnar loop*?
3. Give the numbers of the ones which are a type of *arch*.
4. Look at your own fingers. What types are your fingerprints?
5. Have your fingerprints always been the same types?

Answers are on page 118.

3 A HOUSE OF THEIR OWN

READING IN CONTEXT

Try to figure out the meaning of the word in italics from the words around it.

Some people like to drink *champagne* at weddings and on other special days.

See the answer on page 118.

Before You Read Building a house is a very big job. Have you ever had a house built for you, or have you known someone who did? What are some of the things that have to be decided before the building can begin? What are some of the problems that can happen?

Glen and Kelly Jones wanted a house of their own.

They were tired of living in a tiny apartment. They were tired of paying rent every week. They were tired of their landlord, Mr. Grant.

Mr. Grant came to their apartment almost every day. He would tell them that he needed to check the lights. Or else he needed to check something in the back hall. He always needed to check something. They knew it was because he didn't have enough to do, but they still felt as if he was checking on them.

"If we had our own house, we wouldn't have Mr. Grant walking in here every day," Glen said.

"If we had our own house, we would have more room," Kelly said. "Then we could have a family."

"Maybe if I got a second job, we could save up the money," Glen said.

"I'll ask my boss for a raise," Kelly said. "Maybe—"

Just then, the doorbell rang. Before Kelly could go to the door, they could hear a key turning in the lock. The door opened, and Mr. Grant came in. "I'm sorry to bother you," he said. "I just need to check on something." He walked into the kitchen. "You had fish for supper," he said. "That's nice. But it sure smells up your apartment, doesn't it?"

Glen looked at Kelly. Kelly looked at Glen. They had to have a house of their own.

They worked hard. They saved every penny they could. They picked out a piece of land they liked. They picked out a house plan they liked. Then they went to the bank to try to get a loan. At last, the bank said yes! Now, they had everything they needed for a house. All they had to do was build it.

"That's the easy part," Glen said. "We just hire some good builders."

Glen found some builders. They could begin soon. "The first thing they have to do," he told Kelly, "is to dig a hole for the basement. They are going to start on March 1st!"

"Oh, that's wonderful!" Kelly said. "Our new house is on its way. Can we go and watch? We should do something special, like they do when a ship is put into the water for the first time. What do they do for a ship?"

"They break a bottle of champagne over it," Glen said.

"Can we do something like that?" Kelly asked.

"If you want to."

"Oh, yes," Kelly said. "I'll get the champagne."

3 • A House of Their Own

At last, it was March 1st. Early in the morning, they left their apartment and drove out to their land. The three builders were already there, with a big **bulldozer**. The bulldozer was running. It was about to dig into the ground.

"Wait!" Glen shouted as he jumped out of the car.

The builders turned to look at him. "What's the matter?" they asked. "Are we in the wrong place?"

"No, this is fine," Glen said. "I want—"

"Well, my wife wants to do something. Kelly, where is the champagne?"

Kelly got out of the car. "I couldn't find any champagne at the store," she said. "So I got something else." She walked over to the bulldozer. "Here's to our new house," she said, and she held up a bottle of milk.

The man in the bulldozer shouted, "No! Lady, wait!" But it was too late. Kelly swung the bottle down onto the bulldozer. Milk and broken glass went everywhere.

The man got out of the bulldozer. He stood and looked at the mess. He shook his head. He could tell that it was going to be a long day.

"Well," he said, "you must be Mrs. Jones. My name is Bob."

"It's nice to meet you, Bob," Kelly said.

The other two builders came over. "Hello," the first one said. "It's nice to meet you. My name is Bob."

"Hello," Kelly said. She turned to the third man. "Is your name Bob, too?"

"No," the man said. "Just Bob."

"You're all named Bob?" she asked. "How do you know who you're talking to?"

The three men looked at each other. Then they looked at her. "Well, Mrs. Jones, it isn't any problem," Bob said. " We don't look the same. And when I say, 'Hey, Bob,' I know I don't mean me."

The three men got to work. Bob got into the bulldozer and started to dig the hole. Glen and Kelly watched for a little while. Then they had to go to their jobs.

They came back at the end of the day. Bob was just parking the bulldozer for the night. He had dug a big hole. But right in the middle of the hole was a huge rock.

"I couldn't move the rock with the bulldozer," he said.

"Oh, no!" Glen said. "Does this mean we're going to have a big rock right in the middle of our basement?"

"No, Mr. Jones," Bob said. "It means we're going to have to blast. We'll do it tomorrow."

"Wow!" Glen said. "Can we come and watch?"

Bob looked at him. "If you want to," he said. "It's your house."

The next morning, Glen and Kelly went back to their land. The builders were there already, getting ready to blast the big rock. Glen and Kelly were careful to stay out of their way. Bob drilled a hole in the rock. Then the Bob with the beard took a long wire and put one end of it into the hole.

It looked as if they were getting ready to blast. Glen and Kelly didn't want to be hurt when the rock blew up, so they went out into the road. That seemed to be far enough away.

Bob took more and more wire off a big roll. He and the other two Bobs began to walk out to the road, laying down the wire as they went. They laid down more and more wire. They went right past Glen and Kelly. They kept going on down the road, farther and farther away from the big rock.

Glen and Kelly looked at each other. Maybe they should move back a little, too. The men had stopped. They were getting ready to blast! Glen and Kelly ran down the road until they were past the men. Boom! The rock blew up into thousands of pieces. Some of the smallest pieces of rock went far up into the air. What if they had gotten hit by one of those sharp little pieces!

The builders walked back to the hole. More slowly, Glen and Kelly walked back behind them. They looked into the hole. Where the big rock had been, there were now a lot of little pieces of rock.

One Bob said to another Bob, "I guess it worked."

The bulldozer pushed the pieces of rock out of the hole. The next day, a truck came to pour cement for the basement walls and floor. Then the builders started on the first floor.

Glen and Kelly went every day after work to see how things were going. It looked more like a house every day!

Kelly watched the men putting away their tools at the end of the day. They looked tired. She felt sorry for them. So the next day, she took a break from work in the middle of the afternoon. She bought a big bag of donuts and took them to the new house.

"Bob!" she called. "Bob! Bob! I brought you some donuts."

One Bob came down a ladder. "Donuts? Did someone say donuts?" he said.

Another Bob came around from the other side of the house. "I love donuts!"

Another Bob came up from the basement. "Hey, thanks, Mrs. Jones!"

They all stood around Kelly and ate donuts, one after the other. When the bag was empty, Kelly went back to work.

A little later, Glen came to see how things were going. Bob's truck was there. But everything was very quiet. No one was sawing wood. No one was hammering nails. No one was moving around at all.

Glen walked into the house. In the living room, the tall, thin Bob had been working on the wall. He was leaning up against it, his hammer in his hand. He was sound asleep.

Glen walked into the kitchen. Bob #2 was curled up in the corner. He was snoring softly.

Where was Bob #3? Glen walked all over the house, looking for him. Then he went out to the truck. Bob #3 was lying on the seat, his hat down over his face.

At supper that night, Glen told Kelly, "I went to the house this afternoon. All the builders were asleep!"

"I thought they looked tired," Kelly said. "That's why I took them some donuts."

"Donuts!" Glen shouted. "No wonder they got sleepy! They shouldn't be eating donuts! They should be building our house! I want them to finish that house just as fast as they can!"

Just then the door opened and Mr. Grant walked in. "Sorry to bother you," he said. "I knocked, but you couldn't hear me. Not with all that shouting."

"Yes, well, what can we do for you, Mr. Grant?" Glen asked. "Did you come to check on something?"

Mr. Grant smiled at them. "I hear your new house is coming along well."

"Yes, it is."

"You wouldn't want your new house to burn down, would you? You wouldn't want it to burn down with you in it, would you?" Mr. Grant asked.

"Why would it burn down?" Glen asked.

"It won't burn down if you have a smoke **detector**," Mr. Grant said.

"OK, we'll get a smoke detector," Glen said.

"Good." Mr. Grant held up a small box. "Here is your smoke detector. You see, I have been renting out apartments for a long time. It was a very good job for me. But now," he said, looking very sad, "things aren't going very well. So I have to

3 • A House of Their Own

find a new job. I am selling smoke detectors. How many would you like to buy?"

"I don't know about this...." Glen said.

"This is a new kind of smoke detector" Mr. Grant said. "Sometimes, a fire doesn't make very much smoke. But the fumes can still kill you. This smoke detector will ring even if there is no smoke. It finds the fumes from the fire before the smoke. This gives you time to get out."

"Glen, I think we should get one!" Kelly said.

"We can get one from the store," Glen said.

"But this one is so much better," Mr. Grant said. "You'll need one for the living room and one for the bedroom. How many other rooms do you have?"

"But—" Glen tried to say.

They ended up with six of Mr. Grant's smoke detectors.

The house was coming along. Glen went every day after work to see it. He talked to the builders a lot and asked them lots of questions.

He told Kelly, "Bob says the house will be all done by the end of May, if everything goes right."

"That's wonderful! We should tell Mr. Grant that we will be moving out."

"Just think! We will only have to pay rent for one more month!" Glen said.

"Then we will have a house of our own. It will be so nice and quiet. There will be no one else around." Kelly gave Glen a big hug. "It will be wonderful."

Kelly was so happy that she left work early and took a big bag of donuts to the builders.

Later, Glen came to the new house. He wanted to talk to Bob about something. He had changed his mind, and he wanted a different kind of floor in the kitchen.

He looked for Bob in the living room. The floor was half done, but there was no one around. There was no one upstairs. He looked outside.

All three Bobs were outside, under a tree in the back yard. They were all asleep.

When Glen got home to the apartment, he told Kelly, "No more donuts!"

"Yes, dear!" Kelly said.

The next day was very hot. Kelly thought about the builders. They were working so hard. They must be hot. Glen didn't want her to take them any donuts. But he hadn't said anything about ice cream.

At lunch time, she left work for a little while. She bought three big boxes of ice cream and took them to the new house.

That afternoon, after work, Glen went to the new house. He wanted to talk to Bob about changing the door in the living room.

When he got to the house, everything was quiet. Very, very quiet.

The next Monday, the builders didn't come to work. Bob called to say that their truck had broken down. They had to fix it. They would be back the next day.

They didn't come on Tuesday. They didn't come on Wednesday. The truck wasn't fixed until Thursday.

While they were gone, Glen had thought of some new changes. He wanted a different kind of windows upstairs. He thought the bathtub should be on the other side of the bathroom, too. On Friday morning, he told Kelly that he was going to stop off on the way back from work to talk to Bob.

Kelly was just happy that they were working on the house again. She wanted to do something special.

She couldn't help herself. She bought them a big bag of donuts.

3 • A House of Their Own

The next week, Glen told Bob that he wanted more room in the kitchen. He asked Bob to move the wall over just a little bit.

The week after that, Glen told Bob that he had changed his mind about the upstairs windows again. He thought it would be nice to have some more built-in closets, too.

The week after that, Glen told Bob that he liked the windows the way they were in the first place. He told Bob to go back to the first plan.

That Friday, Bob #1 was sick and couldn't come to work. Bob #2 and Bob #3 decided to take the day off, too.

"This is terrible!" Glen shouted at Kelly. "I want them to finish this house as fast as they can! How can they finish it if they take a day off? How can I talk to Bob about changing the lights in the living room?"

The next week, Bob called to say they had to wait for more wood for the new kitchen floor Glen wanted. "We should get it next week," Bob said.

Glen told Kelly, "They just can't seem to get things done fast enough. The house isn't going to be ready. We won't be able to move in this month."

"But we have to!" Kelly said. "Mr. Grant has already rented our apartment to someone else! They will be moving in on June 1st!"

"We'll have to move in, then, even if the house isn't ready." Glen said. "It will be good to be right there so that I can talk to Bob every day. That should make things go faster."

"We'll have a roof over our heads," Kelly said, and Mr. Grant won't be there."

On May 30th, Glen and Kelly took the day off from work. They rented a truck. They had packed everything in their apartment into boxes. They began to put the boxes in the truck.

Mr. Grant came out to watch them. "Today is your big day?" he said. "Isn't that nice! Let me help you with those boxes."

"No, that's all right," Glen said. "Thank you anyway."

But Mr. Grant picked up a box. "This is heavy!" he said. He put it down again, hard. "What's in here?"

"That's our dishes," Kelly said.

"I didn't know dishes were so heavy," Mr. Grant said. "I'll just check to see if they're OK." He opened the box. The dishes all had newspaper around them. He began taking the dishes out of the box. He took the newspaper off all the dishes. He piled them up on the floor around the box.

When the box was empty, he stood up. "They're all OK," he said. "Is there anything else I can do to help you?"

Kelly looked at the dishes all over the floor. "No, thank you, Mr. Grant," she said.

Glen and Kelly spent the night in the new house. They couldn't unpack anything yet. The kitchen wasn't ready because of the new floor. The bathroom wasn't ready because the bathtub had to be moved.

The floor in the bedroom was only half done. They couldn't set up their bed. They had to sleep on the floor.

But they were still happy. "It's all ours," Glen said. "There's no one here to bother us."

Kelly woke up early the next morning. At first, she just lay still, her eyes shut. She thought she was still in their old apartment. Then why was someone walking around by her head?

She opened her eyes. There were feet right next to her head. A man's feet.

She look up. There was Bob, his hammer in his hand. He was looking down at her. "Good morning, Mrs. Jones," he said. "I know you want this floor finished, so I thought I'd get an early start."

3 • A House of Their Own

"That's nice of you," Kelly said softly. She got up very quietly so that she wouldn't wake Glen. She knew he needed his sleep.

Then Bob got to work.

Glen and Kelly were eating their breakfast. They had to shout to hear each other over the hammering upstairs. "I hope they hurry up and get done!" Glen shouted.

"So do I!" Kelly shouted back.

Glen went off to work. Before Kelly went to work, she told Bob, "I left some ice cream in the freezer. You can have all you want."

That afternoon, Glen came home to the new house. He went upstairs to see if Bob had finished the bedroom floor.

The floor was all done. Bob had even set up the bed.

He was asleep in it.

"No more donuts and no more ice cream!" Glen shouted at Kelly as he left for work the next morning. "Can't you see that you're keeping them from getting this house done? I've asked them to change the railing on the stairs, and I want to be sure they do it today!"

"All right, all right," Kelly said. "I won't give them anything."

The builders changed the railing on the stairs. They changed the door on the bedroom closet, too. Then they were ready to put in the new smoke detectors. That afternoon, Mr. Grant brought them over to the new house. He brought a gift for Glen and Kelly, too. He left it on the kitchen table for them.

It was a big bag of donuts.

Glen and Kelly felt as if they were living with Bob. Bob was in the upstairs hall every morning. Another Bob was hammering in the kitchen while they ate breakfast. Another Bob was outside the window, putting on the trim. "I feel as if Bob is everywhere," Glen said. "I feel as if I'm going crazy."

"There, there," Kelly said. "They will be done soon."

49

"I want them done now!" Glen shouted. "I can't stand it any more! Not any more! Not one more day!"

Just then, Bob walked into the room. "I just wanted to tell you," he said. "I think we'll be done next week. If there aren't any more changes."

"That's wonderful," Glen said.

Day by day, the week went by. Every day, the builders worked on the house. But Bob #2's children got sick. And Bob #3 hurt his leg. And they couldn't get the wood for the upstairs window trim. And Glen thought it would be nice if they put another closet in the downstairs hall.

"I think we'll be done in just one more week," Bob said.

"That would be nice," Glen said.

"One more week, if everything goes OK," Bob said. "If anything else needs to be changed, it could be two weeks."

Three weeks later, the house was done.

The builders packed up their tools. They got in their truck and went away, with one last bag of donuts.

"It's so quiet! And no one is asleep!" Glen said.

"What do you mean?" Kelly asked.

"Never mind. I'm just glad no one is here but us," Glen said. "Just you and me."

The doorbell rang. "Our first visitor!" Kelly said. "Who could it be?" She ran to the door and opened it. There stood Mr. Grant.

"I just thought I'd come to see your house," he said. He walked in and headed for the kitchen. "I just wanted to check on your new smoke detectors."

Glen showed Mr. Grant where the smoke detectors had been put in. Then he showed Mr. Grant around the house. Then he showed him right out the front door.

"There! He's gone!" Glen told Kelly. "We never have to think about him again!"

"That's right, dear," Kelly said. "Now you just sit down and rest. I bought some nice fish for our first supper."

She started to cook the fish. As the smell of the cooking fish went through the house, the smoke detectors started to ring. First, the one in the kitchen. Then, the one in the living room. Then, the one in the upstairs hall. Soon, all six were ringing.

Glen and Kelly had forgotten to ask Mr. Grant how to shut them off.

Comprehension Check

Pick the best answer for each question.

1. Glen and Kelly wanted a new house for many reasons. Which one of these was not a reason for building a new house?

   a. They thought they would save money.

   b. They would not have a landlord to bother them.

   c. They would have more room.

   d. They would have someone to check on things for them.

2. Why did Kelly break a bottle of milk on the bulldozer?

   a. She thought people broke a bottle of milk on a ship when they put it in the water.

   b. She thought the bulldozer was a ship.

c. She couldn't find any champagne, so she thought milk would be fine.

d. She thought she was buying champagne, but it turned out to be milk.

3. Why do you think the builders didn't tell Glen and Kelly to get out of the way when they were getting ready to blast the big rock?

   a. The builders hoped that Glen and Kelly would be hurt.

   b. When the builders got out of the way, they thought that Glen and Kelly would move, too.

   c. The builders didn't think that the blast could hurt anyone.

   d. When the builders got out of the way, they didn't know that Glen and Kelly were there.

4. Why did Kelly keep taking food to the builders?

   a. She was just trying to be nice to them.

   b. She thought it was part of her job.

   c. She thought they didn't have enough to eat.

   d. She wanted to slow down the building.

5. Why did Glen keep asking the builders to make changes in the house?

   a. He wanted his new house to be just right.

   b. He thought the builders were doing a bad job.

   c. He didn't really like the house plan they had picked out.

   d. Kelly kept asking him to make the changes.

3 • *A House of Their Own*

6. Which of these did not happen when Glen asked for changes?

    a. It took longer to build the house.

    b. It cost more to build the house.

    c. Glen lost a lot of time from his job.

    d. The builders got so tired of it that they left.

7. At the end of the story, why were Glen and Kelly still thinking about Mr. Grant?

    a. They wanted him to help them bring their boxes in from the truck.

    b. They needed him to tell them how to shut off the smoke detectors.

    c. They wanted him to come to visit them every day.

    d. They didn't like being all alone in their new house.

8. Bonus Question! Which of these is the best man with a hammer?

    a. Bob

    b. Bob

    c. Bob

    d. Mr. Grant

Answers are on page 118.

Cambridge Reader

Reading Tips: Ending (er)

Long words are sometimes made up of a shorter word and an ending. Look at these words:

smaller = small + er

faster = fast + er

The *er* ending means *more*.

The work is going *faster*.

faster = more fast

The *er* ending has another meaning. Look at these words:

builder = build + er

bulldozer = bulldoze + er

What is the meaning of *er* in these words? Look at these sentences:

I want to *build* a house. I will hire a *builder* to do the work.

I need to *bulldoze* this land. I will get a *bulldozer* to do the work.

The *er* ending means *the person who, or thing that, does the work*.

You can think of many other words with this ending.

The person who can *paint* a house is a *painter*.

A thing that can *grind* meat is a meat *grinder*.

3 • *A House of Their Own*

There are a few rules about putting on endings. If the word ends with an e, you take off the e before you put on the ending.

bulldoze ⟶ bulldoze +er ⟶ bulldozer

If the word ends with one vowel and one consonant, most of the time you have to double the consonant before you put on the ending.

big ⟶ big + g + er ⟶ bigger

What is the meaning of the *er* ending in each sentence? Circle the right meaning.

1. Bob is tall*er* than Glen.

   more

   a person who does the work

2. The small*er* pieces of rock went high in the air.

   more

   a thing that does the work

3. She put the ice cream in the freez*er*.

   more

   a thing that does the work

4. When they were packing, Glen and Kelly didn't think Mr. Grant was a very good help*er*.

   more

   a person who does the work

5. Glen wanted a house because he was tired of being a rent*er*.

   more

Cambridge Reader

a person who does the work

6. Glen and Kelly thought it would be much nicer to have their own home.

more

a thing that does the work

Answers are on page 118.

READING FOR BACKGROUND:
Floor Plans

Before you can build a house, you have to make a plan. The plan will show what the house will look like. It will show how big each part of the house will be, what each part will be made of, and how it will all fit together. The builders will use this plan as they build the house.

There are many different kinds of plans. Some show what the house will look like on the outside. Others show how the basement will look. One kind that is very useful is the floor plan. The floor plan shows how big each room will be and how you will get from one room to the next.

Look at this floor plan. Some words are made shorter to save room. RM means "room," and KIT means "kitchen." DN means "down." The lines where it says DN show where the stairs to the basement will be.

The numbers in the rooms show how big the rooms are. The living room is 23′ 6″ x 12′ 0″. This means that the living room will be 23 feet 6 inches long, and 12 feet zero inches wide. The lines at the top of the plan show how big the whole house will be. The house will be 28 feet and 10 inches wide. The house will also have a carport, which will be 12 feet wide.

3 • A House of Their Own

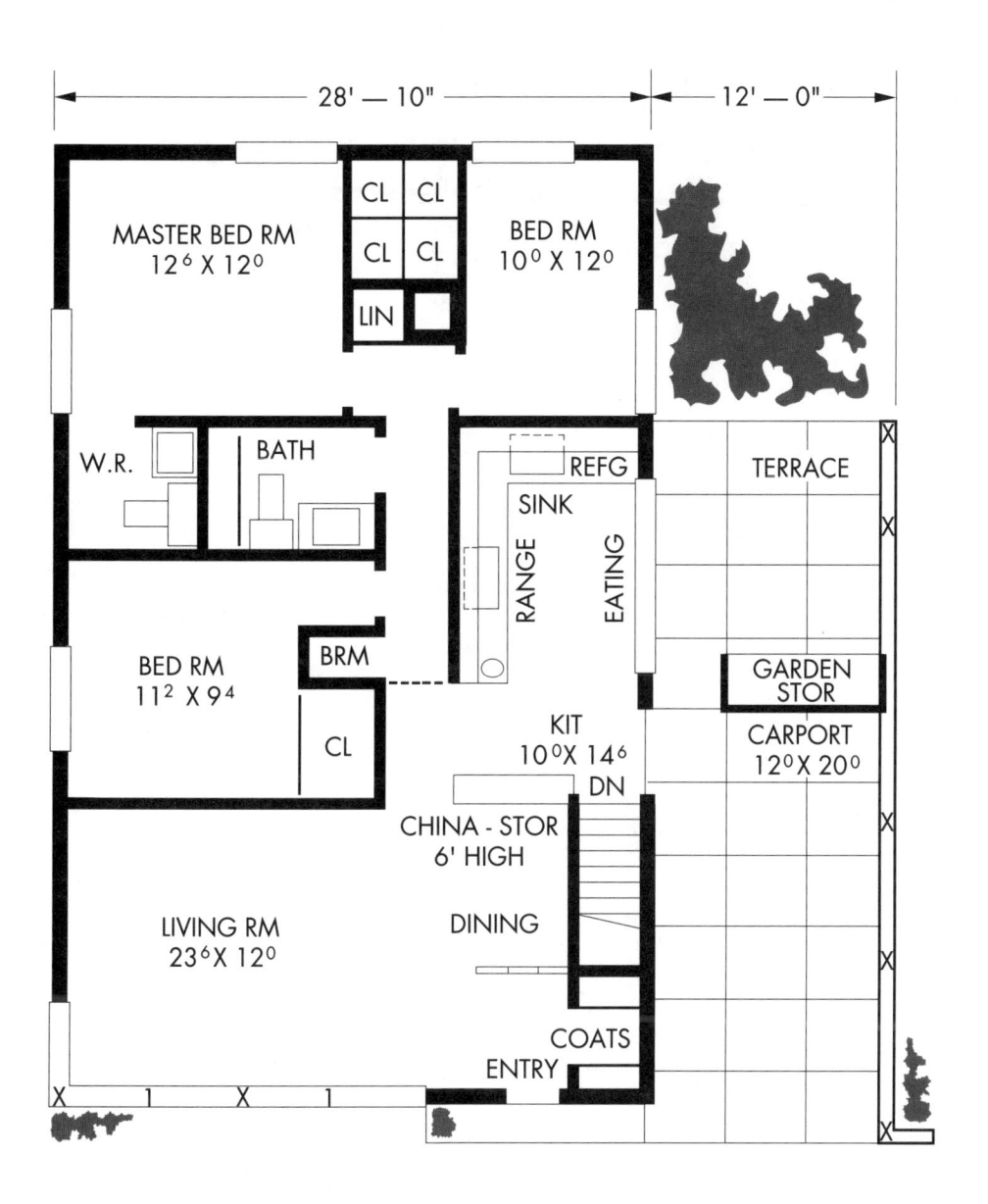

Use the floor plan to answer these questions.

1. How many bedrooms will this house have? _____
2. How big will the kitchen be? _____
3. How big is the biggest bedroom? _____

Cambridge Reader

4. Can you tell what CL is short for? _____

5. What room would you have to go through to get from the front door to the kitchen? _____

Answers are on page 118.

4 THE HOUSE THAT WASN'T THERE

READING IN CONTEXT

Try to figure out the meaning of the word in italics from the words around it.

They went to the old *cemetery* to look at the headstones of people who had died a long time ago.

See the answer on page 118.

Before You Read Do you believe in ghosts? No? Well, do you believe there are some things in the world that no one can explain?

Rob and Linda were on their honeymoon. They had packed their things into Rob's old car, and now they were driving across the state.

Rob pointed at the sky. "I don't like the look of those clouds," he said. "I think it's going to rain."

"Oh, dear," Linda said. "How long will it take us to get to our motel?"

"I don't know. Take a look at the map."

"OK." Linda got out the map and looked at it. "Where are we, anyway?" she asked Rob.

Rob looked in front of him at the road. "I don't know. *You* have the map. What does the map say?"

"Rob, the map isn't any good if I don't know where we *are*!"

Just then, the rain hit them. It was raining hard. The rain pounded on the roof of the car, and on the hood. The windshield wipers could hardly keep up with it. Rob was having a hard time seeing the road.

"We can't go very far in this rain," Rob said. "We'd better stop in the next town. Look at the map and tell me what the next town is."

"But Rob, I don't know where we *are*!"

Suddenly, there was a bright flash of lightning, and a terrible crack of thunder. Rob held tightly to the steering wheel. Linda covered her ears with her hands.

"Oh, Rob, let's get out of here!" Linda cried.

"I'm trying!" Rob said.

Flash! Crack! Flash! The lightning was all around them. The wind was blowing hard now. The branches of the trees were waving around. It seemed to be getting darker by the minute.

Flash! Crack! Crash! A big tree fell down across the road right in front of them. Rob stepped hard on the brakes. By the time he got the car stopped, the branches were touching the hood.

"Rob, turn around! Quick! We've got to get out of here!"

"Don't worry, Linda. We'll be all right." Rob turned the steering wheel hard. The car began to turn around.

Crack! Crash! Another tree fell a few feet behind them.

They were trapped.

It was dark now, as dark as night.

"Oh, Rob!" Linda cried. What were they going to do? They had to get out of there. But where could they go?

Suddenly, he saw a light shining through the trees. It hadn't been there a moment ago. What was it? The lightning flashed again, and he could see a house. The light was shining out the window.

"A house! Linda, there's a house over there!" Rob said.

4 • The House That Wasn't There

Linda lifted her head. "Where?" she asked, looking around. "I don't see a house."

"Right there!" Rob said, pointing. "Can't you see the lights? It's right there!"

"I still don't see anything," Linda said.

"Well, never mind, *I* see it. Come on. Let's get out of the car and go over there. We'll be safer in the house."

They got out of the car. The wind pushed at them, roaring like an animal. The trees waved around them, creaking loudly. The rain pounded down on them. Rob took Linda by the hand and pulled her toward the light he had seen.

Linda pulled back a little. "Why is it so dark out? It's only 3:00! Where is this house? I still don't see it!"

"It's right in front of us, silly!"

"But—"

She saw Rob lift his hand as if he was knocking on a door. Suddenly, there *was* a door. There was a house.

"It must have been there all along," Linda thought to herself. "Why didn't I see it? It *must* have been there . . ."

Rob knocked again. They waited.

Slowly, slowly, the door opened.

Two tiny old ladies stood looking at them. One was holding open the door. The other was standing in back of the first one, as if she wanted to hide. They both wore long, long skirts, right down to the floor, and they had **shawls** held tightly around them. They looked scared, but they were smiling bravely.

"Hello," Rob said. "My name is Rob, and this is my wife, Linda. Our car is stuck—there are trees across the road. Could we come in?"

"Oh, my, yes," the first lady said. "Come in, come in, out of the rain. I've never seen such a storm! Do come in, and dry yourselves off by the fire. Maybe we can find you some dry clothes to put on."

Rob and Linda stepped into the house. It was very small inside, and dark. The only light came from two kerosene lanterns, and a fire crackling in the fireplace. Rob and Linda hurried over to the fireplace and stood in front of the fire.

"Boy, you sure were lucky to have those lanterns," Rob said. "Your electricity must have gone out as soon as the storm started, right?"

"Pardon me?" the first lady said. She looked **puzzled**. "The lanterns? Yes, I suppose we are lucky to have such good lanterns."

The other lady was coming in from another room with some dry clothes. She held up a dress. "Try this on, my dear," she said to Linda. "You are bigger than I am, but this will have to do until your clothes dry." She looked at the clothes Linda was wearing with that same puzzled look. Then she held up a pair of pants and a shirt for Rob. "These belonged to my husband," she said. "He was about your size."

Linda and Rob went into the other room to change. The old lady's clothes were strange. "These pants don't have a zipper," Rob told Linda.

Linda looked closely at the dress. "I think this dress was all made by hand," she said. "She must have had this dress for a long, long time."

"There, that's better," the first lady said as Rob and Linda came back into the living room. "Now we can hang your own clothes by the fire to dry. My name is Miss Melanie Tinker," the first lady said. "This is my sister, Mrs. Sarah McCall. She came to live with me after her husband died in the war."

"He died at sea," Mrs. McCall told them. "He was too old to fight, but he was taking a ship full of food to the soldiers in the War Between the States."

"What is the War Between the States?" Rob thought to himself. "She couldn't mean the war in Vietnam. She must have meant World War II. Or maybe even World War I. These ladies look like they're about a hundred years old."

Linda was looking at Rob. He had that same puzzled look on his face, as if something wasn't quite right.

"We've already had our supper," Miss Tinker was saying, "but we'd be glad to get you something to eat."

"Oh, no, that's all right," Rob said. He looked at his wristwatch. It was only 3:30. "We're not hungry. But we would like to use your phone, if it's still working in this storm."

Miss Tinker looked at him sadly. "I'm sorry, son," she said. "I don't hear very well any more. What is it that you would like to use?"

"Your phone," Rob said loudly.

Miss Tinker looked at her sister. Mrs. McCall shook her head. "I'm sorry," Miss Tinker told Rob. "I don't think we have a *phone*."

"She must mean she doesn't know if it's working or not," Rob thought to himself. "People *know* if they have a phone or not."

No one spoke for a moment. All they could hear was the wind blowing outside, and the rain pounding against the windows.

"Well," Mrs. McCall said brightly, "even if you aren't hungry, maybe you'd like some tea. I'll go heat some water." She headed into the kitchen.

"Can I help you?" Linda asked. She started to follow Mrs. McCall into the kitchen. But when she got to the doorway, she stopped.

Everything in the kitchen was old. The table and chairs were made of wood. The open shelves held jars and cans of food— but the cans looked so old-fashioned. Nothing looked as if it had come from a supermarket. Linda watched as Mrs. McCall got water from a pump at the sink. Then she put some wood into the wood stove. When she opened a wooden chest to get out a pitcher of milk, Linda saw a block of ice keeping the food cold.

The kitchen looked like a room in a **museum**. But the two old ladies were *using* these things! They were really living like this!

Linda stepped into the room and looked around more closely. All the things in the kitchen *looked* old. But a lot of them weren't old. The chest with the ice looked brand-new!

"I see that you're looking at our new icebox," Mrs. McCall said. "We were so pleased to get it. Until we got it, we had to keep our food down in the cellar if we wanted to keep it cool. This is so much handier." She went over to the shelf and got down a teapot.

Linda just shook her head. Why would anyone want to put food down in the cellar to keep it cool? And now they had to keep putting blocks of ice into an icebox. "Don't you ever wish you had a refrigerator?" she asked.

Mrs. McCall looked at her. "A what, dear?"

"A refrigerator," Linda said again.

"What is a refrigerator?" Mrs. McCall asked. "Is that some kind of new-fangled tool for a kitchen? No, I think we can do quite nicely without it."

Linda just looked at her, with her mouth hanging open. Had Mrs. McCall really asked what is a refrigerator?

"Now, if you would just put some tea in the pot," Mrs. McCall said. "I'll get the cups. Do you and your husband take sugar?"

"Yes, please," Linda said. She began putting tea into the pot. "This is starting to seem like a dream," she thought to herself. "Maybe I'll wake up, and I'll find out I've just been dreaming."

They brought the tea into the living room. "This is just lovely," Miss Tinker said as she poured the tea into the cups. "We don't get visitors very often." She turned to Mrs. McCall. "We haven't even seen Mr. Roth lately, have we, Sarah?"

4 • The House That Wasn't There

"No, not for more than a week. His horse is lame," she told Rob and Linda, "so it's hard for him to get here."

Rob and Linda looked at each other. Rob looked down at his wristwatch. It now said 4:10. Then he looked out the window, at the nighttime darkness.

Something was wrong here. Something didn't make sense. But what?

He looked around the room. The light from the fireplace shone on the old ladies' faces. They looked so sweet as they sipped their tea. They looked as if they were so happy to have visitors. How could anything be wrong?

When they were all done with their tea, Miss Tinker stood up. "It is past our bedtime," she said. "The storm does not seem to be letting up, and it is far too late for you to think of going on. We have a spare room upstairs. My sister and I would be very happy to have you spend the night."

"Oh, Rob, I don't know," Linda said. She wanted to get out of there. Even though it was still storming outside, she wanted to get away from that house.

Rob felt the same way. "Oh, we couldn't put you to so much trouble," he said. He started to get up. "We really should be going . . ."

"Oh, no, you really must stay," Mrs. McCall said. "It's no trouble at all."

"But—"

"It's no trouble at all," Mrs. McCall said again as she hurried up the stairs. "I'll have your bed made up in a minute."

"I'll lend you one of my nightgowns," Miss Tinker told Linda. "I'll bring you a pitcher of warm water, so you can wash up."

"But—" Rob tried again.

"Your room is all ready," Mrs. McCall called from upstairs. "Just bring a candle with you when you come."

Before they could say anything more, Miss Tinker took Rob and Linda upstairs. Soon they were tucked up in a big brass bed, under a hand-made quilt.

They were not sleepy at all.

"This place scares me," Linda whispered. "I know that some people like to live as if it's the old days. But this is different. Rob, Mrs. McCall said she doesn't even know what a refrigerator *is*!"

"I know what you mean. It didn't sound as if Miss Tinker knows what a phone is," Rob said. "Maybe they just never go anywhere."

"But they talked about having visitors. There was someone named Mr. Roth. *He'd* know about phones and refrigerators."

"No, Linda," Rob said. "Remember? He couldn't come this week because *his horse was lame*."

"Oh, Rob." Linda began to cry. "I don't know why, but I'm scared."

Rob held her tight. He didn't want to tell her that he was scared, too.

It was a very dark, cold night.

After a long time, they fell asleep.

Linda was the first to wake up. Before she opened her eyes, she lay still. She could hear birds singing. At first she thought she was at home in her own bed. Then she remembered the wedding, and the long drive in the car, the storm . . . and the house with the two old ladies.

Her eyes flew open. Rob was beside her. But where were they? The sun was shining on them, and there were tree branches all around them. There were pine needles almost touching her face.

She sat up and looked around her. Now she could see that they were in Rob's old car, in the back seat. But how did the pine needles get there?

4 • The House That Wasn't There

"Rob, wake up!" Linda called. She shook him until he opened his eyes. "Look at the car!"

Rob sat up. "My car!" he yelled.

A big pine tree was lying across the front of the car. The hood and windshield were all smashed in. Right where they had been sitting . . .

"Rob," Linda said.

"Linda."

"If we have been sitting in the front seat—"

"We would have been killed," Rob said.

They sat for a minute without saying anything.

"Rob," Linda said.

"Linda," Rob said, "how did we get into the back seat?"

They looked at each other.

"Rob," Linda said softly, "do you remember the house, and the two old ladies?"

"Miss Tinker and Mrs. McCall," Rob said. "Yes, I remember them too."

"We were in their house, remember? I had Miss Tinker's nightgown on."

Rob looked down at her clothes. "But now you have your own clothes on. And I don't remember leaving the house and coming out to the car. Do you?"

"No," Linda said. "I don't know how we got into the car."

"Do you think we were walking in our sleep?" Rob asked.

"Maybe we weren't really at the house," Linda said. "Maybe we were dreaming."

"But how could we both have the same dream?" Rob asked.

Just then, they heard the sound of trucks, and men's voices.

"Look at all these trees!" someone was saying. "It's going to take a while to get this road cleared."

"Hey!" another voice shouted. "There's a car in here! There's a tree on top of it!"

Cambridge Reader

"Oh, no! Is there anyone in it?"

"Come and help me! Look at this! If there was anyone in the front seat, they're dead!"

The men were trying to climb over the tree on top of the car. Rob and Linda could see the branches around the car waving as the men worked their way into the car. Rob rolled the window down. "We're here!" he called. "We're all right!"

The men got to the car and looked in through the windows.

"You're OK? I can't believe it! *Look* at this car! If you'd been in the front, you'd have been crushed!" Quickly, the men helped them get the door open and get out.

"We *were* in the front," Rob said as soon as he and Linda were out of the car. "We were driving along, and this storm came up—"

"It was some storm!" one of the men said. "There are trees down all over the place!"

"—and a tree came down right in front of us," Rob went on.

"Then, before we could turn around, another tree came down in back of us. We were trapped."

"Then what happened?" the men asked.

Rob looked at Linda. "Well, we got out of the car, and— Well, we went to that house over there..." He pointed toward the old ladies' house. But somehow he knew, before he even looked.

There was no house.

"There aren't any houses around here," one of the men said. "The nearest house is about five miles that way."

Linda held tightly to Rob's hand. "We don't really remember anything after we got out of the car," she said. "We were pretty scared. I guess we just got in the back seat of the car and went to sleep."

"Yes, I guess that's what we did," Rob said.

"Well, it's a good thing you got out of the front seat," the man said. "We'll get this tree cut up and see how bad your car is."

68

"Wait. Can I ask you one thing?" Rob said. "What time did the storm end?"

"Well, let's see. It started at about 3:00, right?"

"And it was pretty well over with by about 6:00 or so. Anyway, I know it wasn't dark yet. We even had a pretty sunset after the storm was all over."

"Thanks," Rob said.

As the men got to work with their saws, Rob and Linda walked toward the place where they had seen the house. There were trees all along the road, with nothing that looked as if a house had ever been there. But when they walked into the woods a little way, they could see a hole in the ground. The hole was large and square and deep, with stones all around the sides. Rob and Linda stood looking down at it without saying anything. They could see that the hole had been a cellar. There had been a house there. A long time ago.

They walked down the road, looking at all the trees that had fallen. As they came around a curve in the road, they saw a small grassy clearing in the woods. As they came nearer to it, they could see that it had five or six old headstones in it. It was an old cemetery.

Rob and Linda walked into the cemetery. There were so few headstones that it didn't take them very long to find what they were looking for. One thin old stone, leaning to one side, said:

Melanie Tinker

August 15, 1801—September 10, 1879

Another stone, right next to it, said:

Sarah Tinker McCall

April 3, 1808—December 21, 1879

"When Miss Tinker died, Mrs. McCall didn't last much longer," Linda said softly.

"I guess there wasn't much for her to live for," Rob said. "She was all alone."

Cambridge Reader

"If Mr. Roth's horse was lame, she didn't have anyone to visit her," Linda said.

"Not even us," Rob said.

Comprehension Check

Pick the best answer for each question.

1. Rob first saw the house when
   a. the rain started.
   b. he and Linda got out of the car.
   c. a lightning flash showed it.
   d. the old ladies opened the door.

2. Why did the old ladies look scared when they opened the door after Rob knocked?
   a. They didn't know who was out there in the dark.
   b. They were afraid that Mr. Roth would try to come in.
   c. They were afraid that their house wouldn't be there.
   d. They didn't want to get wet.

3. There were many things about the old ladies that puzzled Rob and Linda. Which of these did *not* puzzle them?
   a. The old ladies did not know what a phone was.
   b. The old ladies used an icebox and not a refrigerator.

4 • The House That Wasn't There

    c. The old ladies wore long dresses and shawls.

    d. The old ladies gave them tea to drink.

4. Why did Linda think that the kitchen looked like a museum?

    a. Everything in it was very pretty.

    b. Everything in it was very old.

    c. Everything in it had cost a lot of money.

    d. Everything in it could not be used.

5. Which of these things must have happened last?

    a. Rob saw the lights of the house through the trees.

    b. A tree fell in front of the car.

    c. A tree fell on the car.

    d. Rob and Linda went into the house.

6. When the road repairmen arrive, Rob and Linda discover that they are in the back seat without knowing how they got there. The men also tell them that there is no house nearby. Which of the following is the best explanation for what happened to Rob and Linda?

    a. The road repairmen are lying—the old house *is* there.

    b. Rob and Linda just forgot that they climbed into the back seat and fell asleep.

    c. Rob and Linda fell asleep in the back seat and dreamed about things that never existed.

    d. Rob and Linda had a dreamlike experience that could not be explained.

Cambridge Reader

7. When Rob and Linda looked for the house after the storm, why did they find nothing but a cellar hole?

   a. The house had blown over in the storm.

   b. The house had been crushed by a tree.

   c. The house had been there a long time ago in the past.

   d. The house had been destroyed by the old ladies.

8. What if Rob and Linda had asked the old ladies what year it was? Which of these do you think the old ladies might have said?

   a. 1775

   b. 1875

   c. 1925

   d. 1975

Answers are on page 118.

Reading Tips: Endings (ly and ful)

Long words are sometimes made up of a shorter word and an *ending*. Look at these words:

tightly = tight + ly
loudly = loud + ly

The *ly* ending means *how it is done*.

Rob held *tightly* to the steering wheel.

The *ly* shows *how* he held onto the steering wheel.

4 • The House That Wasn't There

The trees creaked *loudly*.

The *ly* shows *how* the trees creaked.

Here is another handy ending:

careful = care + ful

handful = hand + ful

Careful means "full of care." *Handful* means "how much you can hold when your hand is *full*."

There is one thing to notice with this ending. When it is used as a word by itself, it has two *l*s on the end: *full*. When it is used as an ending, there is just one *l*: careful.

These two endings can be used together to make even longer words, like this:

carefully = care + ful + ly

He picked it up care*fully*.

How did he pick it up? In a way that was *full* of care.

These endings are easy to write. Because they start with a consonant, you don't have to change anything. Just put the ending right on the end of the word.

Put the right word into the blank in each of these sentences:

quickly	softly	sadly
spoonful	bravely	cupful

1. She wanted to be quiet, so she spoke _____.
2. He wanted to get there as _____ he could, so he ran.
3. I'm going to have a cup of tea. Would you like a _____?

Cambridge Reader

4. "My husband died in the war," she said
   _____ .

5. She put a _____ of sugar into her cup of tea.

6. He set out _____ int-o the storm to help the people who were trapped in their car.

Answers are on page 119.

READING FOR BACKGROUND:

Time Lines

A time line shows when things happened. When you look at a time line, you can see which things happened first or last. You can also see which things happened at the same time.

This time line shows when some things were invented, or made for the first time. It also shows some dates in the history of the United States.

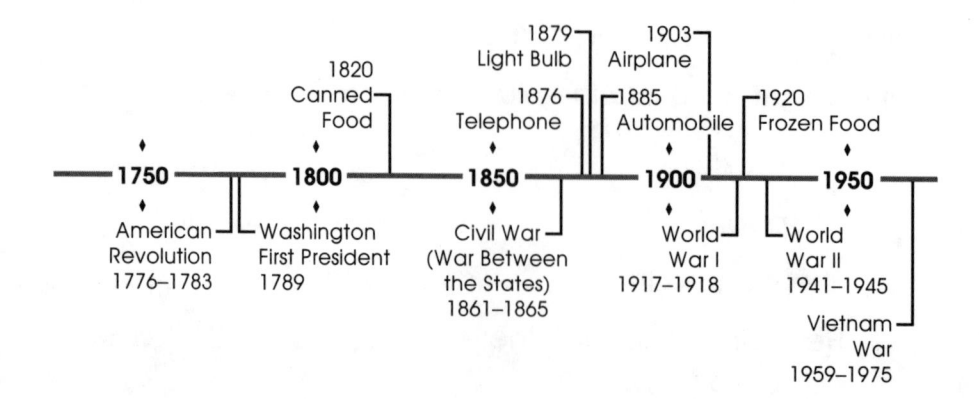

```
                                    1879┐  1903┐
                           1820     Light Bulb  Airplane
                           Canned┐   1876┐ ┌1885    ┌1920
                           Food    Telephone Automobile  Frozen Food
                             ♦        ♦      ♦ ♦        ♦
───1750─────────1800────────1850─────────1900─────────1950───
      ♦           ♦           ♦            ♦    ♦
   American ┘└ Washington   Civil War ┘   World ┘└ World
   Revolution  First President (War Between  War I    War II
   1776–1783   1789           the States)    1917–1918 1941–1945
                              1861–1865
                                              Vietnam ┘
                                              War
                                              1959–1975
```

4 • The House That Wasn't There

Use the time line to answer these questions.

1. Which was invented first, the telephone or the light bulb? _____

2. What year did the Civil War begin? _____

3. Did George Washington become President before or after the Revolution? _____

4. Do you think that soldiers in World War I might have been given canned food to eat? _____ What about frozen food? _____

5. Which war was the first one during which airplanes were used? _____

Answers are on page 119.

5 COLD WATER

READING IN CONTEXT

Try to figure out the meaning of the word in italics from the words around it.

He saw the *jellyfish* floating in the water, like little blobs of jelly.

See the answer on page 119.

Before You Read Have you ever been to the ocean? On a warm, sunny day, it's a beautiful place to be. But you have to be careful. If you aren't careful, what are some of the things that could happen?

Mark had never seen the ocean. He had always wanted to see it.

This year he had two weeks off from work. He packed up his family and headed for Maine to see the ocean.

He didn't know that it might be the last thing he would ever do.

Mark and his wife, Alice, found a motel near the beach. They spent two happy days there with their little girl, who was five years old. They lay in the sun, played in the sand, and looked for shells. Sometimes, they went in the water, but they didn't stay in for long. It was so cold!

"I didn't know the ocean would be so cold," Alice said.

5 • Cold Water

"Maybe it's cold because it's so big," Mark said. He looked out across the water. "You can just see forever. Look at those little islands way out there. I love it!"

"Well, *I* don't!" a little voice said behind him. "It's too cold, Daddy. It's too cold to swim, and I'm tired of playing on the beach. I'm tired of the ocean."

"Well, now, Jessa," Mark said. "There are lots of other things to do at the ocean. How about a boat ride? We could rent a boat. Then we could go look at those little islands."

"Oh, Daddy, can we? Can we go in a boat?"

"I don't know," Alice said. "I don't think it would be safe. You don't know anything about boats, and you don't know anything about the ocean. You might hit a rock or something like that."

"Don't worry," Mark said. "I'll get someone to take us. I'll get someone who knows the way around. Then we'll be safe."

But they weren't.

The next afternoon, they headed down to the dock. A man was waiting for them with his boat. "This is Stan Wood," Mark told his family. "He's going to take us out."

Alice looked down at the boat. "Isn't it kind of small for all of us?" she asked.

"It'll hold you all just fine," Stan said. "It's a good little boat, and it has a good outboard motor. Come on down and get in." He showed them how to put on their big orange **life jackets**. Then he untied the boat from the dock and started the motor. The boat pulled away from the dock and headed for the open ocean.

The little boat rode over the waves, up and down, up and down. The sun shone brightly on the water. It was a lovely day. Mark felt great. Jessa was happy. Even Alice began to relax and have a good time.

The boat pushed farther and farther away from the land. The dock and the beach began to look very small and far away.

They were coming closer to one of the islands. They could see hundreds of birds sitting on the rocks. Jessa saw a seal. The big sea animal was lying in the sun. Alice smiled at Mark. This boat ride was turning out just fine.

They passed the island and headed even farther out. "We're getting so far from land!" Alice said.

"Don't worry. Mr. Wood knows what he's doing," Mark said. But he felt worried, too. They couldn't see the dock now at all.

Suddenly, it was very quiet. The motor had stopped. "Rats!" Stan said. "Something is wrong with it *again*!" He got out some tools and began to work on the motor.

The boat rode the waves, up and down, up and down. The boat seemed very small all alone in the middle of miles and miles of water. Mark tried not to look at Alice. He didn't want to know what she was thinking.

"Well, I'm sorry about this," Stan said. "This happens sometimes with this motor. I know I can get it fixed, but it would be a lot easier if I could set it up on land. I'm going to row us to that island over there. Then you can walk around while I'm working on the motor."

"OK," Mark said. It would be good to get onto land again, he thought.

Stan put a pair of oars into the boat's **oarlocks** and started to row. When they got to the island, they got out and pulled the boat up on the rocks. Alice and Jessa went off to look around the island, while Mark helped Stan take the motor off the boat.

"We'd better take the motor up there," Stan said, pointing higher up the beach. "The tide is all the way out now. Soon, the water will start to come back up. These rocks will all be under water down here."

5 • Cold Water

They carried the motor up the beach. They had to go slowly over the wet, slippery rocks. "Now I'll go back to the boat for my tools," Stan said. As he turned, his foot slipped on a wet rock. He fell back. His hands grabbed at the air. His head hit a big rock, and he lay still.

"Mr. Wood!" Mark shouted. He hurried down the rocks to where Stan was lying. Was he dead? No, he was still breathing. But he looked bad.

Mark ran up the beach. "Alice! Come here! Quick!" he shouted. "Mr. Wood fell and hit his head! He's out cold!"

Alice came running, Jessa right behind her. "What are we going to do? We don't dare move him, not if he has hurt his head! But he doesn't look good. Do you think he's going to die?"

Jessa started to cry. Mark gave her a hug and said, "Don't worry. He'll wake up soon. You put our jackets on him to keep him warm. I'll see if I can fix the motor. Everything will be all right. You'll see."

But he couldn't fix the motor.

Stan didn't wake up.

They were stuck on the island. There were no ships in sight anywhere.

The tide was starting to come in.

Mark said, "We've *got* to get help."

"How do you think we're going to do that?" Alice asked.

"We can row the boat," Mark said.

"All the way to shore? That would take so long!" Alice looked down at Stan. "I'm afraid if we move him that much, he'll die."

"You stay here with Jessa and take care of him," Mark said. "I'll go alone. That will be quicker."

"But you don't know how to row!"

"I watched Mr. Wood do it. It can't be too hard." Mark was already pushing the boat down to the water. He climbed in and put the oars into the oarlocks. "Give me a good push," he called to Alice. "I'll be back as soon as I can."

Mark found out quickly that rowing a boat was harder than it looked. The waves kept pushing him back to the island. It was all he could do to keep the boat from crashing against the rocks. Then he began to get the hang of it. The boat began to pull away from the island. Alice and Jessa looked smaller and smaller, standing on the shore.

Mark headed for the first island they had passed not long ago. It seemed like days ago! He rowed and rowed. He rowed for what seemed like an hour, or two hours. That island didn't seem to be getting any nearer. In fact, he saw that the waves were pushing him right by it. But at least he should be getting closer to shore. He turned in his seat to see how far away the island was where his family was waiting. It was just a tiny speck in the water, far away.

For a few minutes, he just sat and rested. Then he pulled on the oars again.

That's when it happened.

One of the oars had slipped out of the oarlock. When he pulled on it, the oar jumped out of his hand. Splash! It fell into the water and began to float away.

Quickly, Mark reached over the side of the boat and grabbed for the oar. He couldn't quite reach it. He had to have that oar! He reached farther and farther—

He almost had it—

Splash! Mark fell into the water. Cold! It was so cold! Mark came up spitting water. His life jacket held him up. But the water was so cold that it took his breath away.

He had to get back in that boat! He grabbed the oar and then tried to swim back to the boat. The boat went up one side of a

5 • Cold Water

wave and down the other. Mark went up and down after it. He swam as hard as he could, but he was gasping for breath. The boat seemed to be moving farther away, not nearer. The wind was blowing it farther and farther away. Then he couldn't see it any more in the waves. It was gone.

It was just him and the oar in the middle of the ocean.

Up and down he went in the waves, up and down. The water was so dark that he couldn't see very far into it. He could hardly see his feet.

How deep was the water here? A mile deep? More than a mile? He thought about the water going down and down below his feet, darker and colder, down and down.

What was down there?

He thought of pictures he had seen of animals that lived deep in the ocean. He thought of the great whales. He thought of sharks with rows of big teeth. He thought of an **octopus** with its long arms—

Something touched his leg.

"Help!" he screamed. "Help! Help!" He kicked his feet hard and tried to swim away. "Help! Help!" The thing kept touching his leg. He reached down to push at it with his hand. It was soft and slimy. Suddenly, he knew what it was: a jellyfish. He had read about them. Some of them were **poisonous**! What about the ones in Maine? Another bumped into him, and another. He could see them now, floating in the water, like little blobs of jelly. He kicked as hard as he could, trying to get away from them.

Pushing the oar in front of him, he swam until he was too tired to go on. Then he just lay there in the water, held up by his life jacket, going up and down in the waves.

He couldn't see the island any more. But he was no closer to the shore. In fact, it looked farther away.

He was being swept out to sea.

The sun was getting low in the sky. In another hour, it would be dark.

He was getting so cold that he couldn't feel his feet. He was hungry and very thirsty. He was too tired to care what happened to him any more. He didn't care if he died. But what about his family? What about Alice and Jessa, all alone on that island?

On the island, Alice sat on a big rock, holding Jessa in her lap. She looked out over the water. Where was Mark? He should be back by now, with help.

They *needed* help. She got up again and bent over Stan. He was hardly breathing. He was so cold, lying on the wet rocks, even with all their jackets over him.

She could see that the tide was coming in. Bit by bit, the water was coming up to where he was lying.

Soon, it would be dark.

Ding! Dong! Mark heard a bell ringing. He thought he must be dreaming. No, there it was again. Ding! Dong! Ding!

Then he saw it. It was a big metal can floating in the water, with a bell on the top. It must be for ships, he thought. Ships must come by! If only he could hold onto it, maybe a ship would find him.

The waves were pushing him toward the can. He reached for it, but it was so big and smooth that he couldn't get hold of it. He tried to let go of the oar, but he couldn't even open his hand. The waves pushed him by the can and farther out to sea.

The sun set.

Bit by bit, it got dark. He could still hear the bell, far away now.

On the island, Alice was watching the tide coming in. The water climbed up the rocks, higher and higher. Soon, it would be touching Stan's feet. How high would the water come?

5 • Cold Water

She couldn't wait any more. She had to move him.

She tried to pick him up, but he was much too heavy for her. If she dragged him over the rocks, it might kill him. But if that didn't kill him, the water would. What should she do?

"Come on, Jessa," she called. "Let's see if we can find something to help us." They walked along the beach, looking at pieces of wood that had washed up in the waves. At last, she saw what she needed: a board. It was long, and it looked strong. She carried it back to where Stan was lying.

Very carefully, Alice rolled Stan onto the board. She bent over him. Was he still breathing? Yes, he was breathing—but slowly.

Now Alice picked up the end of the board. She tried to pull it up the beach.

It wouldn't move.

She pulled harder. She pulled with all her might. But it was no use. Stan was too heavy.

Too tired to pull any more, she sat down beside the board. She saw that the water was already over Stan's feet.

Mark was dreaming that he was riding down a steep hill in a car. Then he woke up. He shook his head. It was just the waves all around him.

Then he dreamed that there was a light shining on the water. It was coming closer and closer. He dreamed that he heard a motor, a big motor.

Was it a dream or was he awake?

The light came closer. Now, he could see that it was a ship. He was saved! They were looking for him! He shouted, "Here I am! Here I am!"

The ship was moving fast through the waves, coming right at him. As it came closer, the bow of the ship was higher and higher over his head.

Cambridge Reader

They should be slowing down, Mark thought. If they aren't careful, they're going to run right over me. Then he knew: they weren't looking for him. They didn't know he was there.

They were going to hit him!

He shouted, but he knew they couldn't hear him over the sounds of the motor and the waves hitting the sides of the boat. He went on shouting anyway. He waved his arm. He picked up the oar he was still holding and waved that.

Suddenly, the sound of the motor stopped. Mark heard voices. "I thought I saw something!"

"What? What did you see?"

"I don't know. There was something in the water. Something flashed in the light."

Mark waved the oar again. "Over here!" he shouted. "Help! Help me! Over here!"

"There's someone out there!" the voice said. Suddenly, a big searchlight was turned on. It came across the water toward Mark. He shouted and waved the oar until the light stopped on him. He could hear more voices shouting and people running. There was a splash of a smaller boat hitting the water. The boat came toward him. Hands grabbed him and pulled him into the boat. As he was lifted out of the water, he felt himself blacking out.

By the time they laid him in the bottom of the boat, he was out cold.

When Mark came to, he was warm and dry. At first, he thought he must be still dreaming. He thought he would wake up again and still be in the water. Then he remembered the ship and the men pulling him into the boat.

Someone was looking down at him. "So you're awake," the man said. "How did you get into the water? Did you lose your boat? Was there anyone else in it?"

5 • *Cold Water*

"Yes, I lost my boat." Mark tried to sit up. "My family! My wife and my little girl are on an island. And the man who owned the boat, too. He's hurt! I don't know which island it is."

"There are no islands near here," the man said. "You must have drifted a long way in the waves."

Mark tried again to sit up. "How can we find them?"

"Look at this chart," the man said. "It's a map of this part of the ocean. Now, where did you start from?" Mark told him the name of the town where their motel was. The man looked at the islands nearby. "We'll start with these," he said. "We have already talked to the **coast guard** on our radio. They are sending a boat to help search, too."

Mark felt the ship turning. Soon, it was speeding through the waves, back toward his family.

Another man brought Mark something to eat. After he ate, Mark started to feel stronger. As soon as he could stand up, he went up on the deck of the ship. He hung onto the railing at the edge of the deck and looked out into the dark. How could they find *any* island, let alone the right one?

Suddenly, he heard a bell ringing. They were passing the big can. "I passed that thing with the bell," he told the men on deck.

One of the men laughed, "That thing is called a bell buoy [BELL BOO ee]," he said.

"OK. Then we're heading the right way," another man said.

The ship pushed on through the waves. Suddenly, the motor stopped. Were they having motor trouble, too?

The men were looking into the dark over the bow of the ship. Mark went to stand beside them at the railing. Suddenly, he saw the black shape of an island in front of them. "Alice!" he shouted. "Alice! Are you there?"

There was no answer.

The men let a small boat down into the water and rowed toward the island. Then Mark could see their flashlights as they searched. He was hoping. But the men came back in the boat. "We couldn't see anyone," they said.

One of them went to check with the coast guard again by radio. "They have checked this island already," he said, pointing at the chart. "Now, they're headed for this one over here. Then they'll go to this one. I think we should head this way."

Mark nodded. The ship's motor started up again, and the ship turned to head out again. They came to another island. Again, the men searched it. Again, they found no one.

Mark felt cold all over. Where were Alice and Jessa? Maybe they were on one of the islands they had stopped at already. Maybe the men just didn't see them in the dark. Or maybe the tide had come up so far that the island was all covered with water.

The men checked again with the coast guard. No luck. They came back to talk to Mark.

"We're going to take you back to shore now. The coast guard will pick up the search again in the morning, when it's light."

"But you can't stop now!"

"I'm sorry, but we're not going to find them this way," the man said. "*If* they're out there."

Mark turned back to the railing. He look out into the dark. His wife and his child were out there somewhere, and he couldn't help them.

Suddenly, he saw a light. It didn't look like a ship's light. It looked like a fire. "Look over there!" he shouted. "What's that?"

The men looked. "Let's go and see!" one of them said. "It's worth a try," the first man said. He started up the ship's motor. The ship turned and headed toward the tiny, faraway light.

5 • Cold Water

On the island, Alice had found some matches in Stan's pocket. She had picked up driftwood from the beach and built a fire. Now she was sitting by the fire, Jessa in her lap. She was leaning up against a rock, almost asleep.

The fire was dying down. Soon, it would be out.

She should put more wood on, she thought. She should keep the fire going. But what did it matter now? Soon, it would be morning. Soon it would start it get light again.

By morning, she thought, Mr. Wood will be dead.

As he lay by the fire, Stan had waked up at last. He could speak to her, but he was so weak, so cold.

She had to do what she could for him. She got up and went into the dark, step by careful step, to try to find more wood.

The ship was moving through the dark toward the tiny light.

"It's going away," one of the men said. "I can hardly see it any more. Now it's gone. It probably wasn't anything. We might as well turn back."

"Please!" Mark said. "Please!"

"We know how you feel," the men told him. "We're sorry."

Mark started to turn away from the railing. Suddenly, the light flared up again. "There!" he shouted. "There it is again!"

"OK! We'll go for it!" the men said. The ship sped toward the light.

Now, they could see the dark shape of an island. They could see the fire clearly now, burning on a little hill. The men put the little boat into the water. "Let me go, too!" Mark said.

They jumped into the boat and rowed to shore. "Alice!" Mark called as the boat touched the rocks. "Alice!"

"Mark! I'm here!" her voice came out of the dark.

"Oh, Alice!" Mark jumped out of the boat and hugged her to him. "Where's Jessa?"

"Right here, Daddy." Now he could see her, standing by the fire. He hurried toward her and picked her up. Then he turned to Alice again. "What about Mr. Wood?" he asked.

"He's there, too," she said. "But I don't know if he will last much longer."

The men from the boat went up to the fire to look at him. One of them hurried back to the ship for a first-aid kit. "I called the coast guard," he told them when he got back. "They're sending a helicopter. It's on its way."

When the helicopter arrived, the crew loaded Stan on board. "We'll get him to the hospital right away. He should make it alive, thanks to you," they told Alice. "You kept him warm with the fire."

"How did you get him up there?" Mark asked. "He must have been heavy."

Alice turned a flashlight to shine on the board that Stan had been lying on. The life jackets were still tied to it. "It took a long time," Alice said. "I floated him up on the tide."

"We're ready to go," the helicopter crew told Mark. "We have room for one more. Do you want to come with us and get checked at the hospital?"

"No, I'm OK," Mark said. "I'll go back on the ship. It's going to be a lovely morning. I want to see the sun rise over the ocean. I also want to finish my boat ride with my family."

Comprehension Check

Pick the best answer for each question.

1. Alice was afraid to go out in Stan's boat for many reasons. Which of these was *not* one of the reasons she was afraid?
    a. She thought that Stan's boat was too small.
    b. She and Mark didn't know very much about the ocean.
    c. She thought the boat might hit something.
    d. She was afraid that Stan wanted to hurt them.

2. From what Stan said, you can tell that
    a. his outboard motor had never broken down before.
    b. his outboard motor broke down often.
    c. he had never used an outboard motor before.
    d. he didn't know how to use a boat.

3. When he fell into the water, why couldn't Mark swim to shore?
    a. He didn't know how to swim.
    b. His life jacket wouldn't hold him up.
    c. The waves kept pushing him away from the shore.
    d. He didn't know which way to go to get to shore.

Cambridge Reader

4. Why did Mark start to think about an octopus?
    a. He thought he saw one in the water.
    b. He was worried about what might be in the water.
    c. He was losing his mind.
    d. He was dreaming.
5. How did Mark find the ship?
    a. He found the can that showed where ships would come by.
    b. He called the coast guard on the radio.
    c. He didn't find the ship. It found him.
    d. He didn't find the ship. He was only dreaming.
6. Why did the men on the ship want to give up the search?
    a. They weren't having any luck, and they were beginning to think that Alice and Jessa weren't really on an island.
    b. They weren't having any luck, and they were beginning to think that Alice and Jessa were already dead.
    c. They were afraid that Mark wouldn't pay them for the search.
    d. They were afraid to be on the ship in the dark.
7. Which of these events happened last?
    a. Alice made a fire of driftwood.
    b. Stan woke up.
    c. The helicopter arrived.
    d. Alice rolled Stan onto the board.

8. Why did Alice put the life jackets under the board?

   a. She tried to make a boat so that she and Jessa could leave the island.

   b. She wanted to keep the life jackets from floating away as the tide came in.

   c. She got the board with Stan on it to float up the beach as the tide came in.

   d. She was playing a game with Jessa to keep her happy.

Answers are on page 119.

Reading Tips: Endings (y to i)

Long words are sometimes made up of a shorter word and an *ending*. Look at these words:

shorter = short + er

rented = rent + ed

These words are easy to put endings on. You put just the ending onto the end of the word.

Some words are a little harder. If a word ends with a *y*, then you have to change the *y* to an *i* before you add the ending. Look at these words:

easier = eas~~y~~ + i + er

hurried = hurr~~y~~ + i + ed

Changing the *y* to an *i* makes the word a little bit harder to read. But if you know that you need to watch out for this

Cambridge Reader

change, then you shouldn't have much trouble reading words that have this change in the middle.

For each sentence, write the italicized word *without* the ending. The first one has been done for you.

1. I am much *happier* now that the sun is shining.

    happy

2. He *tried* to grab hold of the big can. _____

3. That is the *funniest* joke I have ever heard. _____

4. Alice was *worried* about Mark. _____

5. They *carried* the motor up the beach. _____

6. Each day was even *lovelier* than the last one. _____

Answers are on page 119.

READING FOR BACKGROUND:

What Makes the Tides?

Every day, all along the sides of the oceans of the world, the tide comes in and goes out again two times. What makes the tides?

We all know about the pull of gravity. Gravity is what makes a rock fall if you drop it. The gravity of the Earth is what keeps us from floating off into space.

The moon has gravity, too. The gravity of the moon pulls on the Earth. The moon's gravity is strong enough to pull the ocean's water a little bit toward one side. That side of the ocean

5 • Cold Water

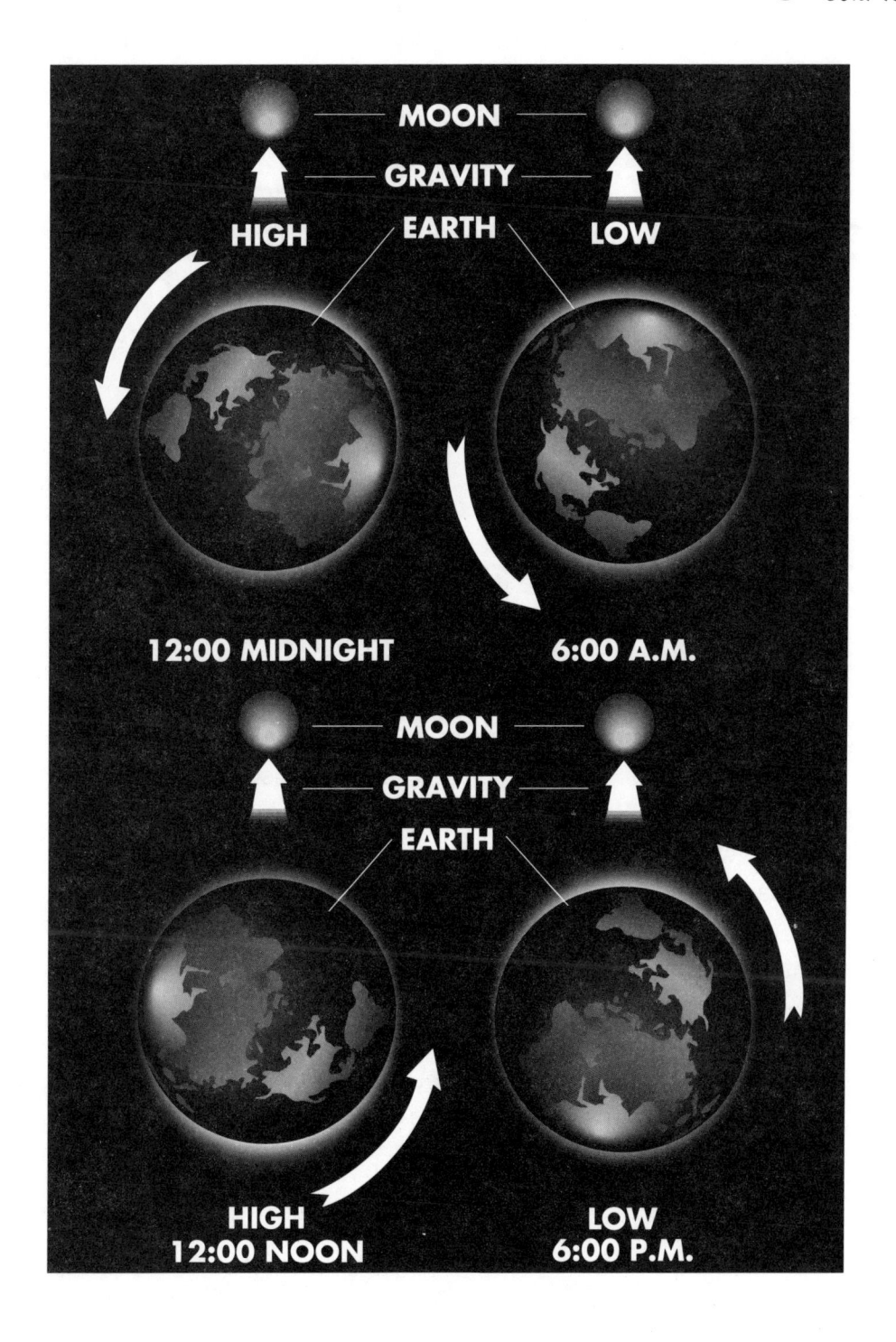

MOON
GRAVITY
HIGH EARTH LOW

12:00 MIDNIGHT   **6:00 A.M.**

MOON
GRAVITY
EARTH

**HIGH
12:00 NOON**   **LOW
6:00 P.M.**

is having high tide. The other side is having low tide because the water has been pulled a little bit away from it.

The Earth turns all the way around every 24 hours. As the Earth turns, each place on the Earth turns with it. When a place is right under the moon, it has a high tide. Then, as the Earth turns, the pull of the moon on the water becomes less and there is low tide.

After a half day, or 12 hours, that place is on the other side of the Earth from the moon. It has a high tide again because the gravity of the moon is pulling the Earth away from the water. So, every place on the ocean has high tide twice a day and has low tide about six hours later, also twice a day.

All water has tides, even lakes. On lakes, the tide rises and falls so little that you can't see it. On the Great Lakes in the United States, the tide is only two inches.

Even along the ocean, the tide is higher in some places than others. This depends on the shape of the coast and on the shape of the bottom of the ocean. It also depends on where on Earth the place is. In some places, the tide rises and falls very little. But on the Bay of Fundy, in Canada, from low tide to high tide, the water rises 50 feet!

In places where the tide changes a lot, people have to change their lives to fit the tides. They need to know when the tide will be high or low.

As the moon moves around the Earth, the times of the tides change a little bit every day. For this reason, it is handy to have a tide chart to know when the tide will be high. In towns near the ocean, you can find a tide chart in the newspaper.

TODAY'S TIDES

Portland high tides	10:09 A.M., 10:16 P.M.
Portland low tides	4:00 A.M., 4:00 P.M.

5 • Cold Water

Kittery high tides	10:02 A.M., 10:09 P.M.
Kittery low tides	4:01 A.M., 4:01 P.M.
Rockland high tides	10:01 A.M., 10:08 P.M.
Rockland low tides	3:53 A.M., 3:53 P.M.

1. At what time in the morning (A.M.) will the tide be high in Portland? _____

2. When will the tide be low in the afternoon (P.M.) in Rockland? _____

3. Which town has high tide first? _____

4. In Portland, at 1:00 P.M., is the tide coming up or going down? _____

Answers are on page 119

6

TIME SHOT

READING IN CONTEXT

Try to figure out the meaning of the word in italics by the words around it.

The astronauts got into the *cockpit* of the space shuttle.

See the Answer on page 119.

Before You Read   Do you remember when the space shuttle blew up? Did you think then about all the millions of things that could go wrong with it? Would you like to travel through time? If you could travel through time, would you go backward or forward? What would you do?

"It's Monday already!" Roger said.

Lynn smiled. "Just two more days until Wednesday—the big day!"

"Yes, just two more days till the space ship is **launched**!"

Five people were eating lunch together. They had been training for this space **mission** for months. Soon, four of them would go into space together. They would be the **astronauts** for the space mission that would begin on Wednesday.

"Are you nervous about the launch?" Ben asked.

"Me? No! Just scared!" Lynn said, smiling.

Roger turned to Chang. "I just wish you were coming with us."

Chang smiled at him. "So get sick or something, Roger. Then I can take your place. No, I'm just joking. I'll get to go on the next mission."

Roger looked at his watch. "Well, I have to go. The Chief wants me at the training center at 1:30."

"He's just keeping us busy. Then we won't think about Wednesday," Lynn said.

"See you later," Roger said. He went out the door and began to walk to the training center.

Suddenly he had a strange feeling. He felt as if he were being watched. He looked around, but he didn't see anyone. "Oh, well," he thought. "I guess I'm just feeling nervous." But he still felt as if someone was behind him, looking at him.

At the training center, the Chief told him to take another turn on the Spinner. The Spinner had a seat on the end of a long frame. The person in the seat would go around in a circle. When it got going, the Spinner could turn around more than 1,000 times a minute. Then the person in the seat would feel the pull of more gravity.

When the spaceship was launched, the pull of gravity would be five times more than the gravity of Earth. If it became too bad, the astronauts might black out during takeoff. The Spinner helped them get ready for the takeoff.

Roger took his place in the Spinner's seat. He saw that the man at the controls was his friend Mike. He smiled at Mike, and Mike smiled back. Everyone was feeling good. Only two more days until Wednesday.

Roger strapped himself into the seat and put on his helmet. When he was ready, he gave Mike the thumbs-up sign, the signal to go ahead. Mike pushed a button on the **control panel**. The Spinner started to move.

Roger went around the room once, twice. The Spinner was picking up speed. Roger leaned his head back against the headrest. Around and around the room he went, faster and faster.

Mike pushed the buttons on the control panel. Now the Spinner was turning 300 times a minute, 400. Roger felt as if he were being pushed back against the seat. This is how it would feel during the takeoff.

Mike pushed more buttons. The Spinner hummed louder and louder as it spun faster. 500 times a minute. 800. Mike pushed one last button. Top speed, 1,000 turns a minute. Mike smiled again. He knew that Roger could take it.

Soon, it was time to bring him down. Mike pushed the red button on the control panel to slow down the Spinner.

Nothing happened.

The Spinner was still turning as fast as ever, with Roger strapped to the seat.

Mike looked at the control panel. What was going on? The Spinner was moving even faster: 1,200 turns a minute. 1,300. 1,400. It couldn't be! It couldn't go faster than 1,000 turns a minute . . . could it? Mike began to panic. What was happening to Roger? He pushed one button after another. The Spinner just kept going faster and faster. It was spinning at more than 1,500 turns a minute! No one had ever gone that fast! Could Roger live through it?

The Chief ran into the room. "There's something wrong in the computer!" he yelled. "The computer is out of control! Shut off the power!" Suddenly the lights went out. Someone had shut off the power to the whole training center. They could hear the humming sound dying away as the Spinner began to slow down. Mike grabbed a flashlight, and they hurried to the Spinner. They knew that Roger would have blacked out. Would he still be alive?

One man grabbed the seat as it came around and slowed it to a stop. The others ran toward the seat to help Roger. Suddenly, they stopped.

Roger wasn't there.

"What's going on, Mike?" the Chief asked. "Is this a joke?"

"No! It's not a joke! Roger was in there!" Mike said.

"So where is he? If the thing was going that fast, well, it could have killed him. But it couldn't make him disappear!"

"He was in there when it started!" Mike said. "I saw him—"

"Mike, I think you've been working too hard," the Chief said. "We're all getting nervous, with the launch only two days away. Now, I'll find Roger. He's around here somewhere. You just get some rest. OK?"

"Yes, sir," Mike said. He walked out of the room as if he were walking in his sleep. The Chief went to look for Roger.

He couldn't find Roger anywhere.

Roger woke up slowly. He knew he had blacked out—but for how long? Slowly, he picked up his head and looked around.

He was still strapped into the Spinner. It couldn't have been very long, he thought, or Mike would have got him out. Boy, did he feel strange. He felt as if he had been turned inside out.

He took off the helmet and looked toward the control panel. He wanted to wave at Mike to show that he was all right. But he couldn't see Mike.

He rested a minute more. Then took off the strap and stood up. Wow! He had to grab onto the Spinner to keep himself from falling. He'd been dizzy before after a ride in this thing, but never like this! He felt sick and weak.

Shaking, he walked toward the control panel. That's strange, he thought. Mike was gone, and all the lights were out. He must have been out cold longer than he had thought. But why would Mike leave him there?

He checked his watch. It was just 2:00, so he'd only been out for a few minutes. He thought he would go back to his room and lie down and rest until supper. But when he walked out of the training center, he saw that it was early morning. The sun was just coming up! Had Mike left him in the Spinner all night?

He looked at his watch again. Had it stopped? No, it seemed to be running all right. *What was going on?*

He walked across the base in the early morning sunshine. There was no one around. Everything was quiet. Where was everyone?

He passed the mission control building. Wait—the parking lot was full of cars! But why? Why would everyone be there at mission control two days before the launch? Or was the launch tomorrow? Roger had never felt so mixed up in his life. He hurried into the building.

The place was full of people. They were hurrying here and there, working at their control panels, watching their computer screens. "They already launched the spaceship!" Roger thought. "They left me asleep in the Spinner, and they launched the space mission without me! *Why?*"

Roger walked slowly through the big room. No one even looked at him. They were all too busy. Something was wrong. "There's trouble," he thought. "There's trouble with the space mission."

He saw the Chief in the middle of a group of people. The Chief was checking a computer **printout** and shouting, something about air. There was something wrong in the cockpit of the spaceship, and the air for the astronauts was getting bad.

No, Roger thought. This is just a bad dream. I'll wake up in my own bed, and the space mission will still be tomorrow. But somehow he knew it wasn't a dream.

Suddenly the Chief looked up at him. "You!" he said. "Where have you been?"

"Me?" Roger said. "I was in the Spinner. You told me to go one last time. I must have blacked out. Then I woke up, and—"

"And you ran away! You were scared, right?" the Chief shouted. "Well, I guess you were right to be scared! If you had gone on this mission, if you were up there with them, you'd be dying right now! Those people are dying! Ben and Anna and Lynn. And Chang! Chang took your place when you ran away! They're dying!" The Chief turned his back on Roger and started to look at the next computer printout.

Roger just stood there with his mouth open. His friends were dying. And the Chief thought he had run away!

"Roger!" said a voice behind him. Roger turned and saw Mike coming up to him. "Roger! Where have you been?"

"I haven't been anywhere!" Roger yelled at him. "You left me in the Spinner!"

"No! You were gone! You took off, right when the main computer made the Spinner go crazy. You took off and left me to tell it to the Chief!" Mike said.

"I didn't go anywhere!" Roger shouted. "I must have blacked out. When I woke up, I was still strapped in the Spinner. I thought it was only a few minutes, but now it's morning. Why did they move the launch up to Tuesday? Why did they go without me?"

"They didn't move the launch!" Mike told him. "It went off on Wednesday, right on time. They went without you because they couldn't find you!"

"You mean it's Wednesday? I was in the Spinner for two days?"

"It's Friday, you jerk! The launch was two days ago."

"Friday!" Roger grabbed Mike by the front of his shirt. "Mike, something has happened! Look at my watch! Look at the time on my watch. Look at the date!"

Mike looked. "It still says Monday, March 14. It says 2:38 P.M.—that's about an hour after I stopped the Spinner. OK, so your watch stopped. So what?"

"Mike, it hasn't stopped. Look, it's still running! Mike, to me, it is 2:38 on Monday!"

"Well, you blacked out—"

"But not for that long! Mike, something has happened. In the Spinner. Mike, it's like I've slipped through time, somehow. I've jumped forward four days."

"Right," Mike said. "You get scared, you run off and get me in trouble with the Chief, and now you want to make up some crazy story about going through time. Roger, we've got more important things to think about! There was a break in one of the cooling hoses. The gas is leaking into the cockpit. Those astronauts are breathing poisoned air! They haven't got much time left! They can't fix the hose and there's no way we can bring them down fast enough to keep them alive! So just get out, Roger. You were too scared to go on the mission. You don't have to stand here and watch them die."

Roger walked away out of the building. He sat down on a bench outside and put his head in his hands. If only it were still Monday! If only the space mission hadn't been launched yet! Then he could get someone to fix that hose. If only it still were Monday . . .

If only there were some way to get back . . .

Roger sat up. He had thought of something. It was worth a try. He jumped up and ran back into the building. "Mike! You have to help me!" he yelled. He grabbed Mike and dragged him toward the door. "I've got to go back to Monday! I've got to get that hose fixed!"

"Let go of me!" Mike yelled. "You really have gone crazy!"

"You've got to help me. You said there was something wrong with the computer on the Spinner. It shot me ahead four days from Monday to Friday. But maybe I can go back! If I can get back to Monday, I can tell someone about that hose. They can fix it so the hose won't break."

"But how can you go back?" Mike asked.

"By making the Spinner run backward."

"That's crazy," Mike said. "Running it backward could kill you."

"I know. But it's the only chance to help Ben and the others. Please help me! Please come!"

Mike came. He kept talking about crazy people, but he came.

They went back to the training center. There sat the Spinner in the dark room. Roger turned on the lights and pushed Mike over to the control panel. "Start it up," he said, pointing at the computer.

Mike turned on the computer. He changed the way it was set so that the Spinner would run backward. Roger got into the Spinner and strapped himself in. It started to move—backward. Faster and faster it went. Going backward felt much worse than going forward, much, much worse. But he could make it. He had to!

Faster— Faster—

He felt himself blacking out.

—and he was waking up in the Spinner. He turned his head to look over at the control panel. No one was there. Had it worked? Or had Mike just run away?

Roger tried to take the strap off. His hands were shaking so much that he could hardly take off the helmet. He was even more dizzy than last time. He felt so weak! It was a long time before he could stand up.

He looked at the clock over the control panel. It was just past 12:00. But what day?

Slowly, he walked to the door of the training center. Mike was coming down the sidewalk with a sandwich in his hand. "Hi, Roger," he said. "You're early. I'm just going to have some lunch. I didn't think you were coming until 1:30." He looked at Roger more closely. "Are you all right?"

"What? Yes, I'm OK. Uh—Mike, what day is it?"

"What *day* is it?" Mike smiled. "As if you could forget. Are you *sure* you're all right? It's Monday! Two days until launch time!"

"It worked!" Roger thought to himself. "It worked! I went back through time!" He wanted to tell Mike all about it. But all he said was, "Thanks. I'll see you at 1:30."

Now what should he do?

He walked slowly to the main building. But just as he was about to go in the door, he remembered. *He was in there already!* He was in there having lunch with the other astronauts. He had gone back a little too far in time. He was a few hours early. This was before he had got on the Spinner.

He hung around outside the building, waiting. Then the door opened, and *he* came out. Roger hid behind the corner of the building and watched *himself* walk down the sidewalk. *He* stopped and looked around, as if he was looking for someone. "That's right!" Roger thought to himself. "I remember that when I came out after lunch, I felt as if someone was watching me. I never would have thought that it was *me!*"

He waited a few more minutes. He wished he could get over feeling so sick. Everything was spinning around him as he walked slowly into the building. He tried to get to the lunchroom where the other astronauts were. He felt so weak. Everything was going black.

When the other astronauts came out of the lunchroom, they found Roger on the floor outside the door.

He was out cold.

The next day, the Chief was sitting by Roger's bed at the base hospital. Chang came into the room. "How is he?" Chang asked.

"The same as yesterday," the Chief said. "The doctors don't know what's wrong with him. He seems to be OK. He just doesn't wake up."

"Are we going to go ahead with the launch tomorrow?"

The Chief stood up. "Yes," he said. "We've got too much riding on it. The mission has to take off right on time. We won't have another chance like this until July. Of course, you'll take Roger's place."

"Yes, sir," Chang said quietly. "I'll be ready."

Wednesday, March 16, had come at last. In the early morning, the astronauts got up and got ready. They ate their breakfast together. They were very quiet. They were all thinking about Roger. They knew how much he had wanted to go on this, but he had still not waked up.

At the mission control building, everything was going well. People were at their places, checking their computer screens. Everything seemed to be A-OK for the launch. The countdown had begun.

The four astronauts walked toward the tall spaceship. They climbed up into the cockpit and took their places. Two hours until launch.

Back in the hospital, Roger began to wake up. He was so dizzy. "Where am I?" he asked.

A nurse hurried to the side of his bed. "Mr. Clark! You're awake! You're in the hospital at the base. Now just rest."

"I feel so dizzy." Roger said. He fell asleep again. The countdown went on.

Suddenly, Roger woke up again. There was something he had to do, something about air.

"Nurse!" he called.

"Mr. Clark?" The nurse hurried over to his bed again. "Are you all right?"

Roger tried to sit up. "What day is it?"

The nurse pushed him softly back down onto the bed. "It's Wednesday," she said.

"Wednesday! That's the launch!"

"Yes," she said. "I'm sorry. I know you were going to be on this mission. But you've been sick. You've been out cold for two days. Mr. Wu had to take your place. The launch will be in just a few more minutes." She pointed at a TV near his bed. "You can watch the launch right here."

"No! No!" Roger shouted. "The air is poisoned!"

"Now, Mr. Clark," the nurse said. "The air in here is just fine."

"Not the air in here!" Roger shouted. "The air in the cockpit! The hose will break! Call the Chief! Tell him to stop the launch! Stop the countdown! Please!" The nurse just looked at him. Roger pulled himself up and put his feet on the floor. He felt so dizzy. So weak. "Hurry!" he shouted.

"Mr. Clark, you must not get out of bed!"

"Get out of my way!" Roger stood up, grabbing for the chair by the bed. "I've got to call the Chief!"

"All right! I'll call him! Just get back in bed!" the nurse said. She picked up the phone. "Mission control? This is the hospital. Roger Clark is awake, and he wants to talk to the Chief. He says there's something wrong with the spaceship. Yes, I know the Chief is busy. But you'd better see if he wants to talk to Mr. Clark."

Roger sat back down on the bed. On the TV screen, he could see the countdown clock. Two minutes. One minute 59 seconds. One minute 58 seconds.

When the clock said one minute until launch, the nurse handed the phone to Roger. The Chief's voice said, "Roger? Look, I'm glad you're awake. If you have something to say, make it quick. This thing is going to go off."

6 • Time Shot

"Chief, stop the countdown."

"Look, Roger—"

"Chief, there's a weak spot in one of the cooling hoses. If it breaks, poison gas will go into the cockpit. There will be no way to stop it. The astronauts will die."

"Now, look, Roger, you've been out cold for the last two days. What do you know about the cooling hoses? You've been dreaming, boy."

The countdown clock on the TV screen said 47 seconds. In a few more seconds, the big engines would begin to fire. It would be too late to stop.

"Chief, I just know. If I'm right and you don't stop the countdown and fix that hose, the astronauts will die. Maybe I'm wrong. But you can't risk it."

44 seconds.

43 seconds. Roger could hear the Chief's breathing on the phone.

42 seconds.

"OK," the Chief said. The phone went dead.

Suddenly, the TV screen changed. A newsman came on, saying, "The countdown has been stopped at 41 seconds. 41 seconds and holding. We have been told that this will not be a long stop. They are making one more check. It looks as if they're opening the cockpit—"

Roger fell back against the pillow. Around him, the room went black.

When Roger woke up again, the TV was still on. It showed the inside of the cockpit. The astronauts were moving around. There was Ben, and behind him was Anna, working on something. They were floating in air. That meant they were in space.

Had they fixed the hose before they took off?

He called the nurse. "What day is it?" he asked her.

"It's still Wednesday. You passed out again for a while, but not so long this time. You must be getting better. I'll go get your supper."

A few hours later, the Chief came in to see him. "I'm glad to see you sitting up," he told Roger. "Are you feeling better? The doctors think you must have had food poisoning."

"Chief, what about the mission?" Roger asked. "Did you—"

"Yes, we checked the cooling hoses. They seemed to be all right. One hose did have a thin spot. It *might* have broken. Maybe. Anyway, we put in all new hoses, just in case."

"Great!"

"But what made you think of the hoses? What made you think there was something wrong?"

"Uh—" Roger said. What could he say? This stuff about going through time sounded crazy, even to himself. "I just got to thinking about them. That's all."

The next day, Roger was strong enough to get up and walk around. But he still kept asking himself if he were going crazy. Thinking that the Spinner could send him through time! Crazy!

Then, on Friday, he began to get nervous. Would the hoses be all right? All through the day, he kept the TV turned on in his room, but there was no bad news. Everything seemed to be going all right with the mission.

"So why do I think that I have been to Friday before?" he asked himself. "I wish I could talk to someone about it. But I can't! I don't want anyone else to know that I'm crazy!"

He was eating his supper on Friday night when Mike came in to see him. "Have you heard the news?" Mike asked.

"What? What? Is there something wrong with the mission?"

"No, no, nothing like that. It's the Spinner. It blew up this afternoon! The Spinner and the computer that runs it. They just suddenly blew up!"

"Was anyone hurt?" Roger asked.

"No. There was no one around," Mike said. "But it looks as if someone came in and turned it on. It looks as if someone was trying to make it run backward or something crazy like that. But who would do that?"

"The way I remember it," Roger thought to himself, "we did."

"There's another thing that's strange," Mike said. "I could swear that you came and got in the Spinner on Monday afternoon. I know you were on the list. I thought you came. I *remember* you being in the Spinner. Then something went wrong with the Spinner, and it went too fast. When I got it stopped, you weren't there. I know *that*. The Chief was really mad at me."

Roger just looked at him.

"But the thing is," Mike went on, "you *couldn't* have been on the Spinner on Monday afternoon because you were here in the hospital. Ben and the other astronauts found you on the floor outside the dining room right after lunch. They brought you here, and you've been here ever since." Mike shook his head. "Maybe I'm just going crazy."

"I don't think so." Roger smiled at him. "I have no way to prove it, but I don't think you're crazy."

The next morning, Roger checked out of the hospital. He was at mission control when the spaceship came in for a landing. He was there to meet the astronauts when they came out.

"It was a great trip," Chang told him. "I was really sorry that you missed it."

Cambridge Reader

"That's OK," Roger told him. "The doctors think I just had food poisoning. They say I can go on the next mission. The Chief says I'll be on the list for July 12."

"That's great," Chang said. "Food poisoning? Wow!"

"It beats air poisoning," Roger thought to himself.

As long as they would let him fly, he would let the doctors think anything they wanted.

Comprehension Check

Pick the best answer for each question.

1. The Spinner was for
   a. helping the astronauts get used to the gravity during takeoff.
   b. helping the astronauts get used to having no weight when they were in outer space.
   c. letting people travel through time whenever they wanted.
   d. showing people how to run a computer.

2. Why did someone cut the power to the training center?
   a. It was the only way to keep the Spinner going for Roger's training.
   b. It was the only way to stop the Spinner and save Roger.
   c. Someone was trying to hurt the space mission.
   d. Someone was trying to hurt the Chief.

6 • *Time Shot*

3. Why did the Chief tell Mike to get some rest?

   a. Mike fell asleep in the Spinner.

   b. He thought Mike was talking crazy when he said Roger had gone through time.

   c. He wanted Mike to train to be an astronaut.

   d. He thought Mike was wrong about Roger disappearing in the spinner.

4. When Roger went through time for the first time, he went from 1:30 P.M. on Monday to

   a. Tuesday

   b. Friday

   c. Saturday

   d. Wednesday

5. After he went back to Monday, why did Roger wait outside the lunchroom?

   a. He was afraid of what would happen if he met himself.

   b. He was afraid of what would happen if the Chief saw him.

   c. He was afraid that no one would believe him.

   d. He had changed his mind about telling the other astronauts.

6. After he went back to Monday, why didn't Roger tell the Chief right away that there was something wrong with the hoses?

   a. The Chief wouldn't listen to him.

   b. Mike told the Chief that Roger was crazy.

111

Cambridge Reader

    c. He blacked out and was taken to the hospital before he could talk to the Chief.

    d. He got mixed up and went to the hospital instead of talking to the Chief.

7. Why didn't Roger tell the Chief that the Spinner was a time machine?

    a. He thought the Chief would be killed if he tried to go through time.

    b. He was afraid the Chief would think that he was crazy and not let him fly the next mission.

    c. He didn't want to get Mike in any more trouble with the Chief.

    d. He had a plan to make a lot of money with the time machine.

8. How did Roger prove to himself that he really had gone through time?

    a. He convinced the Chief to inspect the cooling hoses.

    b. He talked it over with the nurse.

    c. Mike remembered that Roger was in two places at once.

    d. The Chief knew that Roger was in two places at once.

Answers are on page 119.

Reading Tips: Endings (y and ness)

Long words are sometimes made up of a shorter word and an ending. Look at these words:

handy = hand + y

lucky = luck + y

The ending *y* turns a word that names a thing, such as *hand*, into a word that tells about something else, such as *handy*.

Some other endings make the change the other way. They turn a word that tells about something into a word that names a thing.

goodness = good + ness

carefulness = careful + ness

Did you see that *careful* is already a shorter word with an ending? *Carefulness* looks like a very long word, but it is just a short word (*care*) with two endings (*full*—shortened to *ful*—and *ness*).

If the shorter word ends with a *y*, the *y* must be changed to an *i* before the *ness* is put on.

silliness = silly + i + ness

Write the italicized word without the ending to finish the sentence.

1. She was a very *lucky* person because she always had good _____.

2. Stop all this *silliness*! Stop being so _____!

3. The boy's mother told him that his bedroom was too *messy*. She told him he had made a _____ in the living room, too.

4. The little girl was all *dirty* from playing in the _____.

5. This store is known for the *freshness* of its food. Everything is very _____

Answers are on page 119.

READING FOR BACKGROUND:
Gravity

We all know that gravity makes things fall to the Earth. It also keeps us on Earth. But it is very hard to say what gravity really is.

Gravity is the force of two things pulling on each other. Earth is very large, so its force of gravity is very strong. The moon is smaller, so its gravity is weaker. This is why astronauts can jump higher on the moon than they can on Earth.

When a space shuttle goes away from Earth, it goes away from Earth's gravity. When it is 210,000 miles away from Earth, the people in it are weightless. They can float about inside the space shuttle.

For this reason, when we talk about gravity and outer space, we can't really talk about weight. We talk about the amount of mass a thing has. This is the amount of stuff the thing is made of. An astronaut may weigh 150 pounds on Earth, be weightless while in space, and weigh only 25 1/2 pounds on the moon. But the astronaut hasn't changed. The astronaut always has the same mass.

6 • Time Shot

Some of the planets are smaller than Earth. They have weaker gravity. If an astronaut visited them, he would weigh less, just as he would on the moon. Some planets are much bigger than Earth. If an astronaut could visit them, he would weigh more. This chart shows how many pounds the 150-pound astronaut would weigh on different planets.

Mercury	57
Venus	136 1/2
Earth	150
Mars	57
Jupiter	381
Saturn	160 1/2
Uranus	135
Neptune	172 1/2
Pluto	7 1/2

1. If a man weighs 150 pounds on Earth, how much would he weigh on Mars? _____

2. If a woman weighs 150 pounds on Earth, how much would she weigh if she could stand on Uranus? _____

3. Which two planets have the same gravity? _____ and _____

Cambridge Reader

4. Which planet must have the greatest mass (and the greatest gravity)? _____

5. Which planet must have the smallest mass? _____

Answers are on page 120.

Answers

1 A LOVE STORY WITH A DOG

Reading in Context   page 1

Ong is the Vietnamese word for *grandfather.*

Comprehension Check   pages 14–16

1. c 2. d 3. a 4. b 5. b 6. a 7. c 8. c

Reading Tips: Compound Words   pages 16–17

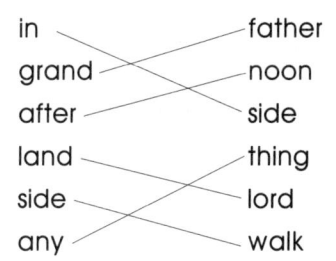

- in — noon
- grand — father
- after — noon
- land — lord
- side — walk
- any — thing

Reading for Background: Dogs   pages 17–18

1. 50 to 75 pounds
2. 14 to 15 inches
3. chihuahua
4. Saint Bernard
5. Irish wolfhound

2 THE KIDNAPPING OF EDWARD R. THURSTON IV

Reading in Context   page 19

IV is put after the name of the fourth person in the family to have that name.

Cambridge Reader

Comprehension Check   pages 33–35

1. c   2. a   3. c   4. d   5. a   6. b   7. a   8. d

Reading Tips: Endings (ing and ed)   pages 35–37

1. hired   2. gasping   3. waiting   4. shouted   5. turned   6. tiring

Reading for Background: Fingerprints   pages 37–38

1. 4   2. 4   3. 1, 2   4. Answers will vary.   5. yes

3 A HOUSE OF THEIR OWN

Reading in Context   page 39

Champagne is a fizzy wine.

Comprehension Check   pages 51–53

1. d   2. c   3. b   4. a   5. a   6. d   7. b   8. Answers will vary.

Reading Tips: Ending (er)   pages 54–56

1. more   2. more   3. a thing that does the work   4. a person who does the work   5. a person who does the work   6. more

Reading for Background: Floor Plans   pages 56–58

1. 3   2. 10 feet 0 inches wide and 14 feet 16 inches long   3. 12 feet 6 inches wide and 12 feet 0 inches long   4. closet   5. living room

4 THE HOUSE THAT WASN'T THERE

Reading in Context   page 59

A *cemetery* is a place where people are buried when they die.

Comprehension Check   pages 70–72

1. c   2. a   3. d   4. b   5. d   6. d   7. c   8. b

Answers

Reading Tips: Endings (ly and ful)   pages 72–74

1. softly   2. quickly   3. cupful   4. sadly   5. spoonful   6. bravely

Reading for Background: Timelines   pages 74–75

1. telephone   2. 1861   3. after   4. yes, no   5. World War I

5 COLD WATER

Reading in Context   page 76

A *jellyfish* is an animal that lives in the sea and looks as if it is made of jelly.

Comprehension Check   pages 89–91

1. d   2. b   3. c   4. b   5. c   6. a   7. c   8. c

Reading Tips: Endings (y to i)   pages 91–92

1. happy   2. try   3. funny   4. worry   5. carry   6. lovely

Reading for Background: What Makes the Tides   pages 92–95

1. 10:09   2. 3:53   3. Rockland   4. going down

6 TIME SHOT

Reading in Context   page 96

The *cockpit* is the part of the space shuttle where the astronauts sit.

Comprehension Check   pages 110–112

1. a   2. b   3. d   4. b   5. a   6. c   7. b   8. c

Reading Tips: Endings (y and ness)   pages 113–114

1. luck   2. silly   3. mess   4. dirt   5. fresh

Cambridge Reader

Reading for Background: Gravity   pages 114–116

1. 57 pounds   **2.** 135 pounds   **3.** Mercury and Mars
4. Jupiter   **5.** Pluto

Glossary

ambulance (AM byoo lanse) a kind of car used for taking seriously sick or hurt people to the hospital The *ambulance* came quickly to the hospital.

astronaut (ASS truh nawt) a person who flies into outer space in a spaceship The *astronaut* returned from his journey into outer space.

bulldozer (BULL dohz er) a big machine for moving dirt The *bulldozer* dug a big hole.

coast guard (COHST gard) a group like the Navy that protects the shores or coasts of the United States that are by the ocean That ship is in trouble! Call the *coast guard*!

control panel (Kuhn TROHL PAN ul) The part of a machine used to run it He stood at the *control panel* of the computer.

detect (duh TEKT) to find out something, or find out where something is; a *detector* (duh TEKT er) is a machine for finding out a special kind of thing A smoke detector will *detect* smoke and tell you if your house is on fire.

launch (LAWNCH) to send a ship into the water for the first time; to send a spaceship into outer space for the first time They will *launch* the space shuttle on Wednesday morning.

life jacket (LIFE JACK it) A short coat without sleeves that will let the person wearing it float in the water A *life jacket* is orange so that the person wearing it can be seen in the water.

mission (MISH un) a trip with a purpose They were getting ready for the space *mission*.

museum (myoo ZEE um) a place for showing things from the past They went to see the 200-year-old tables and chairs in the *museum*.

oarlock (OR lahk) the part of a boat that holds an oar that the person uses to row a rowboat; a rowboat has an oarlock on each side, one for each oar The *oarlock* turns as a person rows the boat.

octopus (AHK te pus) an animal with eight long arms that lives in the ocean He was scared that he might meet an *octopus*.

plant (PLANT) the building or group of buildings where people work. He worked in a *plant* that made car parts.

poisonous (POY zuh nuhs) something that can hurt or kill by putting a hurtful or deadly liquid into the body of another living thing Some animals and plants are *poisonous* to people.

printout (PRINT owt) a paper put out by a computer that prints what you have written on the computer He was reading a long computer *printout*

puzzle (PUZ zul) to confuse; also, something that confuses This problem will *puzzle* you! OR: What happened between those two people is a *puzzle*.

rescue (RES cue) to help or save someone who is hurt or in danger; also, people who are trained to do this The firemen *rescued* the people from the burning building.

shawl (SHAWL) a square of cloth used to cover a woman's shoulders She put a *shawl* around her shoulders.

Vietnam (vyet NAM) a country in Southeast Asia The people of *Vietnam* are called Vietnamese.